914.16

VIOLENCE IN IRELAND

VIOLENCE IN IRELAND

A REPORT TO THE CHURCHES

CHRISTIAN JOURNALS LIMITED, BELFAST

VERITAS PUBLICATIONS, DUBLIN

First edition 1976 by Christian Journals Limited, 2 Bristow Park, Belfast BT9 6TH, and Veritas Publications, Pranstown House, Booterstown Avenue, Co. Dublin.

Revised edition 1977.

ISBN 0 904302 27

Made and printed in Ireland.

Contents

Foreword

This report comes from the fifth Working Party appointed by the Irish Council of Churches/Roman Catholic Church Joint Group on Social Questions. The Joint Group is itself a committee authorised and instituted by the Irish Hierarchy of the Roman Catholic Church and the Irish Council of Churches. The function of the Joint Group is through the efforts of a number of working parties appointed by it to advise the Hierarchy and the Irish Council of Churches concerning their role in Irish society with special reference to social problems. (Previous Reports : Drug Abuse, 1972; Housing in N. Ireland, 1973; Teenage Drinking, 1974; Underdevelopment in Rural Ireland, 1976).

The problem of violence in Ireland is of urgent concern to us all. It not only threatens individuals but also the whole fabric of society. In commending the Report and its conclusions to the Hierarchy, the Council and the Member Churches of the Council, we express the hope that it will be given very serious consideration by all who are concerned for the future well-being of the people of this island.

On behalf of the Joint Group, we express our thanks to the members of the Working Party and officials for the work they have done.

GERARD McCONVILLE
WILLIAM ARLOW
Joint Secretaries

Preface

As Joint Chairmen, we commend this report to the study of the Joint Group and through it to the Christian Churches in this country.

We pay tribute to the members of the working party who have given freely of their time, experience and counsel in order to produce it. Invitations to join the working party were, we understand, extended to some others who for various reasons were unable to accept membership. A few who did accept the invitation were for good reasons compelled to withdraw at various stages.

We are anxious to pay tribute to Mrs. Joan Nesbitt and Miss Ruby Stickel of the Irish Council of Churches Secretariat who uncomplainingly typed several interim drafts of the report. For a considerable period Miss Kathleen Kelly, a member of the working party, acted as Honorary Secretary until professional duties made it impossible for her to attend meetings over a number of months. During this time Miss Teresa Murphy was an efficient and willing substitute. The working party is grateful to both of them. Finally we must refer with particular gratitude to the unwearying skill and patience of Dr. Stanley Worrall, who was solely responsible for gathering together and formulating the various drafts. Without his work the report would have been a much inferior document.

+CAHAL B. DALY

R. D. ERIC GALLAGHER

Joint Chairmen

Introduction

It was inevitable that the problem of recurring violence in Ireland should call for the attention of the Joint Group on Social Questions. Believing that, irrespective of the past (and indeed of the present), the Churches have an obligation for the future which they dare not evade, the Group, after consultation with the Hierarchy and the Council, invited us to work to the following terms of reference :

'Recognising that violence or the threat of violence is and has been recognised by different groupings in Irish society as to them an acceptable method of changing the structures of Government (or of preventing such change):

'1.   To enquire into the moral, physical and economic effects of violence or the threat of it on those who resort to it, on those against whom it is or has been used and on the community generally;

'2.   To indicate to the Churches how they may best educate their members in the social and political implications and application of the Christian gospel so that they may promote the achievement of a society acceptable to the great majority of the people by means which rule out recourse to such violence.'

The Working Party met in plenary session fourteen times and numerous meetings of smaller groups and consultations were held. In its approach to its task, the Working Party decided to invite the general public North and South to contribute written evidence on personal experiences of violence and its effects. Letters were inserted in the national and provincial press, to which few replies were received.

In addition a member of the Working Party, a trained sociologist, carried out an important piece of personal research into attitudes and experiences in two Belfast Secondary Schools, in so-called 'ghetto' areas. Use is made of his findings in Chapter 2 (pp. 53-55).

Early in its work the Party realised the need to be careful in its understanding of the meanings to be attached to the word 'violence' and to other words and phrases frequently used in the discussion of it. Members were alert to the dangers inherent in the emotional or emotive use of terms. There is a place in human affairs for the use of 'force'; we should like to keep the word 'violence' for a use of force that is not justifiable, whilst realising how difficult it may be to determine what is or is not justifiable. There are then at least two different ways of drawing the line between 'force' and 'violence'. The distinction can be based on the authority behind the action: it is argued that the state has the right to use such force as is necessary to restrain wrong-doers; the consequent conclusion is that for anyone else to use force is unlawful and therefore constitutes 'violence'. Such a distinction raises the grave difficulty that the state is capable of acting unjustly or may seem to some to be based on a usurpation. Can no force be used against it legitimately ? The answer often seems to depend on the political viewpoint held. Alternatively the distinction can relate mainly to method: there is a

9

constructive use of force, in which the minimum interference is made with persons and property, in order to attain one's end—a strike, for example, or an arrest. There is, on the other hand, a destructive use of force, in which persons and property are considered of small account in relation to the end to be achieved. Such destructive force may be exercised by the State, through its agencies, as the long history of persecution and oppression shows, or it can be exercised by those who seek to resist the state and in so doing appear to claim exception from the ordinary moral restraints on conduct.

In this report 'violence' always has a pejorative sense and the word is not employed as synonymous with 'force'. The pejorative sense derives partly from the idea of 'illegitimacy' and partly from the idea of 'destructiveness'. We believe that the State must avoid, to the utmost possible extent, any element of unnecessary destructiveness when it uses force to restrain the violent. We believe also that the use of force by those who oppose the State is more difficult to justify and therefore more easily constitutes 'violence' on grounds of illegitimacy. For example, to apprehend an individual for interrogation is a use of force by the State but is in most cases violent kidnap on the part of anyone else; but the method of interrogation, or detention for a period beyond immediate necessity, might turn the State's use of force into 'violence', in which case it should be classified as such. With these considerations in mind our working definition of 'violence' is 'the unjustifiable use of force'—and opinions among both writers and readers will vary about how justification is to be assessed.

The report and recommendations which follow do not pretend to be a complete treatment of the problem either in general or in its particular Irish manifestations. There are several factors that require more detailed attention and treatment than the members were either competent or had time to give. They would hope that others coming after may deal fully and adequately with those gaps.

Note on Terminology

Power. This word appears to be the basic term. 'By power is meant the capacity to initiate action and to bring about change. Power is exercised both by individuals and by groups, and it is of many kinds, military power, economic power, political power and so on. There cannot be truly human persons or truly human communities without power . . .' (John Macquarrie, *The Concept of Peace*, S.C.M., 1973). Power is effective and frequently used and needed) in decision making. Power is needed for the development of personality and community, to achieve basic needs which have been identified as including love and security, new experience, praise and recognition, responsibility'. (Mia Pringle, *The Roots of Violence and Vandalism* 1973).

Conflict. 'Conflict occurs when individuals or groups or even ideas with contradictory claims come into confrontation with e a c h other' (Macquarrie, op.cit.). Conflict in this sense is not necessarily harmful. It is an ingredient in the peace and development of a society or an individual. When conflict gets out of hand, human existence is distorted; conflict then becomes destructive instead of creative.

Force. Force is pressure, physical or moral, used to resolve conflict. (Rational persuasion is not, of course, 'pressure' in this sense). The use of force to achieve political or ideological aims may have the effect of revealing latent conflict. The unjustifiable use of force is violence.

Aggression. Aggression occurs when one side precipitates a situation of conflict by initiating the use of force against the other. If the side initiating action to change the *status quo* is the victim of obvious injustice the term aggression is only appropriate if the action is irresponsible or excessive.

Violence. This is the central term about which it is important to be clear. Some definitions are too narrow. For example : 'Violence is the initiation of physical assault or offensive action' (S. Hook 'Violence' in *Encyclopaedia of the Social Services* 1934). Others are too wide : 'I refuse to make any classic distinction between violence and force . . . It is impossible to distinguish between justified and unjustified violence, between the violence that liberates and the violence that enslaves' (Jacques Ellul, *Violence,* S.C.M. 1969). It is essential to distinguish between the lawful use of force and the unlawful use of force, which is violence.

N.B.—The Working Party is concerned about the loose use of the phrase 'institutional violence', by which is meant, properly, injustice committed or maintained by the use of force by the authorities. We believe that this term should be used with great caution. Otherwise, the point can easily be reached where those engaged in action against the State can represent their activities as morally comparable to those of the authorities. But 'any state has to use force for the restraint of its anti-social members; but if this force is kept down to minimal levels, we would not normally call it violence' (Macquarrie).

1. Violence in Ireland

The Historical Perspective

Physical force and violence, and the threat of them against persons and property to achieve political and social ends, has been a recurring feature of life in Ireland for centuries. To that extent its roots lie deep in Ireland's past. And that past cannot be divorced from the problems of political and economic power and in particular from the presence in Ireland of a political authority backed by military power which was seen by many as alien. The British authorities, whenever in past centuries the situation became difficult, used various devices of force or violence to maintain their control over the island; and on the other hand there has been in each generation one or more groups of Irishmen prepared to use similar methods to challenge the British authority and expel the British presence.

Another deplorable legacy of the former colonial history of Ireland has been the use of religious affiliations for political ends. Britain, like most imperial powers, whether Protestant or Catholic, frequently used religious division as an instrument of imperial policy. Down to the middle of the nineteenth century, there was religious discrimination and denial of political rights and economic opportunities to Roman Catholics and to dissenters. This

13

had two evil consequences which remain sadly with us. Firstly, the use of religion for political ends, practised in this country by Britain, became an element in Irish politics and has remained such long after the British colonial regime as such ended and long after it had been abandoned in Britain. Secondly the struggle of Catholics for religious liberty went hand in hand with the struggle for national independence. This led to a tendency to identify nationalism dangerously with Catholicism. It imparted a quasi-religious fervour and flavour to Irish nationalism. Parallel with this has been, on the other hand, an identification of British loyalty with Protestantism and a tendency to regard the British link as the necessary protection of the Protestant religious heritage. Denominational labels could thus easily become synonymous with political allegiances; while, in parallel fashion, the political history of Ulster became frequently coloured with religious emotions. In evaluating the place of religious differences in the Northern Ireland problem, the legacy of the colonial past cannot be ignored.

In the early 17th century English and Scottish settlers came in large numbers to the North of Ireland. Their descendants have now had their homes in this country for as long as any English-speaking men have lived in North America. The difference in religions, resulting from the fact that this migration occurred after the Reformation had taken place in Britain, played a part in preventing the gradual assimilation of the old and new populations that would otherwise have been likely to take place. The Protestant population assumed that British control of the island would be permanent and, when it was questioned, felt that their security and interests depended on its continuance. In the late 19th and early 20th centuries the British began to see the need to concede at least a measure of self-government to Ireland and it was the resistance to this of the Protestant people, now identifying themselves as Unionists, that led to partition. A profound fear of subjection to an alien culture underlay this resistance. On the other hand it is important not to underestimate the degree to which partition was seen as an affront and an injustice by those who aspired to a democratic and independent Ireland. It seemed to many in the Catholic community, numbering some 70% of the population of the island, that the country had been mutilated in order to meet the relatively frozen position of the group that was dominant in the North, a group that sought to maintain both the British link and the Protestant ascendancy, from both of which Irishmen had struggled hard to free themselves. The power-struggle had left a situation with which neither side was wholly satisfied. The Nationalist or Republican interest was left with twenty-six counties and the Unionist interest with six, the latter in fact comprising about one-third of the country's population and resources. This area, however, contained a large minority of Catholics, who not only shared with those south of the border the general sense of disappointment that Ireland had been divided, but also had to face the problem of their position as citizens of the Northern State. In large measure they withheld co-operation and this seemed to the Unionists, who had accepted partition, to be unreasonable and irresponsible. They saw it as a deliberate self-exclusion from the community, while in course of time the Nationalists came to see themselves as the victims of discrimination.

Each side held the other to blame for the deep division that existed in the State.

This historical background, although it can be summarized in this matter-of-fact way, has induced on both sides a depth of feeling which it is difficult for the outside observer fully to appreciate and which is undoubtedly strengthened by the religious dimension. On the one hand there is the profound inner conviction that the British presence has for centuries brought nothing but suffering, humiliation and neglect to the Irish, a conviction that does not always lose its potency when somewhat qualified by objective historical study. On the other hand there has been an attitude based on the strange amalgam of superiority and insecurity that characterizes a minority when it is maintained as an elite by external power. The use against the British presence, whether in the whole island or since 1920 in Northern Ireland, of methods held by their users to be a justifiable use of force on behalf of their nation, has seemed to the unionist community not only to constitute illegitimate violence but also to be a direct menace to which it must respond with counter-violence if British protection wavered or failed. We have seen in recent years how very strong remains the determination to maintain an identity distinct from that of the Irish majority and to demand political institutions that will guarantee the distinction. The British, who for so long remained in Ireland to secure their own interests, now see themselves constrained to remain when otherwise their best interests might be served by withdrawal.

The foregoing suggests with some qualifications that force or violence and the threat of them for political and social ends in Irish society has been on the nationalist side a response to the British military and political presence in Ireland, and the outcome of frustration caused by a feeling of alienation from the political regime by which they were governed; and has been on the part of the Protestant settlers and their descendants a response to the sense of threat and insecurity that seems always to have been with them. To see Irish violence, both nationalist and unionist, as a response to circumstances is in no way to condone or to justify it. In recent times public opinion in democratic countries has become uneasy about the use of certain forms of force even to uphold the authority of the State. Such measures as internment without trial and interrogation under torture; such practices as house searches and the use of plainclothes agents; such events as 'bloody Sunday': all these have been strongly questioned and in many cases unequivocally condemned by law-abiding citizens. This is a measure of the growth of humane sentiments and brings into sharp relief the methods used against authority by modern terrorists. For if there is a hesitation to countenance apparently harsh methods by the State in upholding public order and the law made by democratically elected parliaments, it is *a fortiori* unjustifiable to support the use of even more barbarous procedures—bombing, assassination, mutilation, expulsion from dwellings and the rest—by self-appointed groups claiming a form of military status and seeking by violence ends for which they are unable to obtain sufficient support at the polls.

At this point the Working Party wishes unequivocally to state its conviction that whatever historical explanations there may be for attitudes taken up by various groups in Ireland, and without prejudice to any legitimate political aim, there is absolutely no justification for the campaigns of violence that have characterized the situation in recent years. Violent action, claimed to be 'military' on the republican side, has lacked any degree of legitimation as an expression of national will, while measures claimed to be defensive taken on the 'loyalist' side should have assumed the form of support for and enrolment in the security forces of the State. However understandable local fears and reactions may have been on certain occasions, the assumption of authority to act for the people by private armies, lacking either official or popular endorsement, has constituted a major threat to civilised life throughout the island.

It is this most recent outbreak of the perennial conflict, occurring at a time when the religious prejudices that aggravate it are outdated and the political issues should be seen in a new and wider framework, that raises acute questions for the Churches in Ireland. How is the occurrence of such an outbreak to be reconciled with the profession of Christian Faith still made by the great majority in the country? How is it to be explained that a people who, by and large, have a deep sense of the religious dimension of existence and have made very great sacrifices for the sake of their Christian Faith have been unable to avoid or prevent the kind of violence that has been experienced in Northern Ireland since 1968? Of course it may be said that violence in Ireland is not an entirely isolated phenomenon, occurring out of relationship to a world context. It is occurring in a world which has seen its most powerful and most developed nations practise the unspeakable savageries of World War II, of Vietnam, of the Middle East.

Violence in Ireland is also affected by the world-wide trend towards increased recourse to violence, whether by individuals or by groups, whether for political ends or in pursuit of criminal or anti-social objectives. Those engaged in violence in Ireland have undoubtedly studied the experience of revolutionary groups in other countries, particularly of those engaged in urban guerilla activity, and have been influenced by their techniques and philosophy of violence. In these aspects, the violence in Ireland of the past decade has not been independent of violence as a world-wide phenomenon. It is true also that only a small percentage of the population has been active in this violence though a large number support the objectives of the violent men on both sides and thus find it difficult to avoid some form of tacit condonation of what is done. And it is not only in Ireland that there are forces in the heart of men which are deeply opposed to the Gospel of Christ and which, when a pretext appears to lend some justification, are prone to express themselves in terrifying forms of evil and destructiveness.

Nevertheless when full allowance has been made for these factors, the Churches in Ireland must ask themselves to what extent a society that has failed to bring to an end the repetitive cycle of injustice and violence that has culminated in the events of the '70's must be said to have failed in its commitment to Christian values. How far have the Churches themselves failed in their preaching and living of the Gospel to bear witness to the full requirements of Christian truth, justice and love? Have not Irish Christians, both individually and as religious denominations, often been found wanting in the extent of their recognition that 'the other side' also possesses these qualities? Concern for sectional interest has weakened the witness of some Christians to their own insights and blinded them to the insights of others. There have been, of course, since 1968 outstanding examples of people bringing Christian values to bear on the situation and there has been a patience and resilience under suffering on the part of very many which undoubtedly springs from Christian faith. Clergy of all denominations have preached love of neighbour and have in many cases helped their congregations to apply their teaching in a relevant way. Two priests have given their lives while ministering to the grievously wounded in the streets. Yet in many quarters, some of them overtly Christian, there has been a refusal to listen to the call to reconciliation. This refusal is no doubt based in many cases on an assessment, right or wrong, of political, material and other interests; but there can be no doubt that it has been given respectability in the minds of many by the polemical spirit which for centuries characterised the relationship of the divided Christian Churches.

Thus there exists a religious dimension to the quarrel. Members of the Working Party are not agreed as to the strength of this dimension, the extent to which it is found in the individual Churches, or the relative importance to be attached to it as compared to social and political factors. What is quite clear, however, is that the more charitable spirit fostered by the ecumenical movement cannot undo overnight whatever harm has been caused by religious division and hostility. Its effects combine today with problems of political loyalty, social justice and cultural diversity to bring about in many quarters a refusal to listen to the call to reconciliation in the face of the tragic events of recent years, to which we now turn our attention.

The current troubles—their course and consequences

The Civil Rights Phase

The troubles that have afflicted Northern Ireland since 1968 began with a series of demonstrations on the part of the Civil Rights Association and the People's Democracy. The objectives of the Civil Rights Association were subsequently defined by the Cameron Commission as being universal franchise in local elections; the re-drawing of electoral boundaries by an independent commission; legislation against discrimination by local authorities and machinery to remedy local government grievances; a compulsory points system for housing allocations; the repeal of the Special Powers Act; and the disbanding of the Ulster Special Constabulary. Behind these specific grievances undoubtedly lay a general feeling on the part of the Catholic population that they were unfairly treated in the Northern Ireland State. Alongside the electoral disadvantages, the allegations of discrimination and the resentment felt at the presence of an auxiliary police force wholly drawn from one community, there was a general feeling of being submitted to a process of Anglicisation in their own country, exemplified in the very limited place accorded to Irish language and culture, the monopoly of broadcasting by the BBC, and the emphasis on British symbols that went well beyond what was customary in Britain itself.

Violence at these demonstrations was limited and sporadic, and when it occurred it was practised against the protest movement rather than for it. It is not surprising that the government should have been suspicious, and the loyalist population convinced, that the demonstrations were anti-partitionist in their inspiration and in their aim. Much in the past history of nationalist agitation and non-co-operation made it difficult for Unionists to believe that this might be in whole or in part a new approach, aimed at justice within the state rather than at its dissolution within a united Ireland. Accordingly every step, official and unofficial, was taken on the assumption—not shared by public opinion outside Ireland—that the new movement was to be identified with the old enemy. The same forces that were resisting, within the government and outside it, Captain O'Neill's attempts to 'build bridges' set about rousing loyalist hostility to change and its advocacy.

The public in Britain saw on television the police action in Londonderry and heard on the radio about riot action at Burntollet. The effect was to increase public sympathy in Britain and elsewhere for the Civil Rights cause and to lead the British government, with its responsibility before international opinion for what went on in Northern Ireland, to press the Stormont government for a more rapid implementation of reform. By the summer of 1969 the stated objectives of the Civil Rights' Movement had been largely met, if not in terms of full implementation at least in terms of an undertaking. No one could say that the minimal amount of petty violence so far committed on the Civil Rights side had forced the hand of the authorities. It was the alerting of public opinion to an apparent injustice which brought about the changes. On the other hand, the use of violence by those determined to maintain the *status quo* may well have contributed to the revival of the deep-seated anti-partitionist sentiment which they feared.

Riot and Intimidation

During the Civil Rights and People's Democracy demonstrations of 1968 and the first half of 1969, the violence had been, as we have seen, minimal. In August 1969 the first deaths directly due to rioting occurred and violence broke upon the people of Northern Ireland with a traumatic effect. The events are thoroughly documented in the Report of the Tribunal under the Chairmanship of Lord Scarman (published April, 1972). In an attempt to ease the pressure on rioters in Derry, Nationalist supporters attacked with stones and petrol bombs police stations in various other towns including Belfast where some major confrontations developed during the nights of 14th and 15th August. Fires were started in business premises and when the Catholic rioting mobs retreated before R.U.C. riot squads, Protestant mobs (said to include 'B' Special police reserves) followed and systematically burnt down a number of streets. Five Catholics and two Protestants were shot dead, while 270 houses were completely burnt out and a similar number damaged, the majority of which were inhabited by Catholics. Many Protestants felt ashamed or at least embarrassed by the ferocity of this attack, while Catholics living in working class areas were badly frightened and proceeded to barricade off their streets.

It was at this point that the Army was called in to support the civil power, and it was in the early days seen as a protective force by many Catholics in West Belfast. This however did not prevent a large scale evacuation of homes in the Falls district, families moving out in large numbers to friends or reception centres in the Republic of Ireland. Some were cared for in Belfast in Catholic Church Halls or Schools, awaiting re-habilitation which frequently took the form of squatting in any empty or partially finished house. This was the commencement of this form of illegal house possession, which was tolerated during this period of chaos, and once established, continued to plague statutory (and private) housing authorities, upsetting their letting plan and pushing those in need of homes further down the waiting list.

The Statutory Welfare Authorities were not prepared to cope with a sudden emergency on this scale. The situation was not made easier for them by the desire of those in the Catholic areas to be cared for in their own institutions. The Welfare Department found that it could best help by sending its officers to organise supplies from these centres. The Supplementary Benefits Commission made grants to those who had furniture and equipment destroyed. This procedure has gone a considerable way to mitigate some of the effects of material damage. There has been no compensation for loss of trade when customers have moved from an area on account of riot conditions. A scheme initiated in 1973 whereby the Government agreed to purchase houses which owners had to evacuate due to the disturbances has helped to cut the loss of those who had to leave their homes and were then unable to sell them.

In 1969, however, money for those who had suffered loss was available from an appeal organised by the *Belfast Telegraph*, amounting to £66,000, to which the British Government added a further £250,000. The Stormont Government also made £50,000 available for immediate relief. These funds were disbursed by a special committee set up by the trustees.

Many of those leaving their homes did so not because of riot damage but because over the succeeding months they were intimidated, being threatened with dire consequences unless they left the district. This had the effect of increasing the existing segregated housing conditions (especially in Belfast). Great hardship was caused, often uprooting families from homes where they had lived for years in harmony with their neighbours.

During the winter of 1969 and into the early months of 1970, civilian vigilantes were able to give some degree of protection particularly in 'mixed' areas, where these still then existed. These peace-keepers came from numerous Peace Committees who were determined not to let the violence spread into their area. At times, clergyman and priest would walk about the streets with well-known citizens in the district, seeking to break up any dangerous looking groups which might be forming. As well as helping to stop a riot developing, Peace Committees were at times able to protect enclaves of housing occupied by a minority who found themselves surrounded by housing occupied by the group dominant in the locality.

By the summer of 1970, these committees tended to run out of steam, and in any case could not cope with the sniper and armed guerilla, or the mobile roving murder gangs. In 1971 and 1972, 'vigilantes' where they existed, were of the one side, trying to protect inhabitants of one street from roving gangs. They used wooden barricades to close off the street. In Catholic areas, the police often could not enter; and, in Protestant areas for this reason, they did not interfere with this breach of the law. In both Catholic and Protestant areas it was easy for a protection group to evolve into a branch of a para-military group. On the Protestant side these organisations grew more out of the frustration and anger of seeing I.R.A. bombing continue, seemingly uncontrollable by the Army, than for the purposes of actual protection of their area.

When, however, fear grips an area, it takes exceptional courage to stand firm and not move home, or to give encouragement to a member of the other side. One sad effect of fear was manifested where neighbours would say—to a member of the other group—'We always were friendly but we think that you had better go for your own safety', and on occasions this really meant 'because we do not want you attracting a fire bomb or gun shots next door to us'.

Evidence has been collected which shows that between August 1969 and February 1973, 8180 families were forced to evacuate their homes. This figure represents only those who contacted official or unofficial agencies and for only ten months' survey spread over the three and a half years. From figures kept by the Belfast Housing Aid Society over the whole period, the researches were able to project figures for the uncovered period and added another 7991 families. They think that 15,000 families may well have moved, representing something between 30,000 and 60,000 or somewhere between 5 and 10% of the population.

Since the publication of the Report, the number of moves has declined—as the segregation of living areas had almost been completed—but there has been a development of intimidation by extremists within their own group, and within their own area.

At this point the difficulty of obtaining witnesses to bring the law-breaker to justice must be stressed as one of the outcomes of violence. Not only does one face danger to one's own person if one enters the witness box to give details about a member of a sectarian or political group, but more subtly the threat can be extended to one's wife and family—a threat which it is unreasonable to expect anyone not to take seriously. This creates a problem for the authorities in their effort to remove the potential murderer or bomber and they resort to evidence heard in camera or given by protected members of the security forces anonymously in a way which does not accord with the best principles of justice. This, in turn, leads to feelings of injustice, or inequality of trials and sentences given.

Bomb and Bullet

The Irish Republican Army which, following the 1956-62 campaign, had given up the policy of violence and was concentrating on a far left political approach which eventually envisaged a uniting of both Protestant and Catholic workers North and South, had been noticeably absent from the August 1969 riots. During the winter, however, a split occurred and a section of the movement not convinced of the political approach broke away to take advantage of the unsettled conditions to try to establish a united Ireland through a disrupted and ungovernable Northern Ireland.

Teenage riots and stone throwing, whether provoked or orchestrated, provided the occasion to infiltrate areas with guns and to snipe against the Army who became 'the invading British forces', the enemy of all true Irishmen.

In response, the Army commenced searching homes for arms. These searches took place almost exclusively in Catholic areas and were not always carried out with care and attention to the families concerned. The para-militaries wore no distinguishing uniform or mark, and the army did not know who was their enemy. The members of the Forces were not trained in police duties and, especially in the case of the paratroopers, were trained in ruthless methods of dealing with the enemy. Brutal methods were on occasion used during searches, especially in areas where a member of the Company had been killed by Provisional I.R.A. gunmen. Inevitable cases of mistaken identity alienated individuals and families not at first ill-disposed towards the Army, and a short but harshly imposed curfew in the Lower Falls Area sharply increased the general hostility. The 'honeymoon' period earlier referred to by the Army G.O.C. General Freeland was over. Such action must be reckoned with as a part of the Northern Ireland violent scene, and almost inevitably the effect was complete Catholic alienation from the Army and a tacit invitation to the Provisionals to take over and act for the area. Another sad effect was that younger and still younger members of the community moved towards the I.R.A. as leaders and heroes who could

28

give them a gun and a new-found aim and challenge in life. This was to be intensified when the Provisionals turned to their bombing campaigns and harmless looking girls and youths became invaluable bomb carriers. When bomb carriers were hoist with their own petard and blown up with their bombs, they were given a funeral with military honours.

Relations with the Forces of Law and Order

One third of the places in the Royal Ulster Constabulary were in 1922 reserved for Catholics; in practice there were never more than 12%. While Nationalists generally regarded the R.U.C. as 'a tool of the foreign power', it must be remembered that a tendency to regard the police as potentially hostile is not uncommon in working-class communities. The feeling that the R.U.C. were anti-Catholic was strengthened at the Civil Rights demonstrations when the R.U.C. used to turn their backs on Loyalist counter-demonstrators to face the Civil Rights supporters, most of whom (though by no means all) were Catholics, or from the Catholic community.

The feeling was exacerbated when the R.U.C. had shown violence in breaking up the Derry demonstration of October 5, 1968, and had then followed this up by entering the Bogside to quell disturbances. In January of 1969, a few policemen again ran amok in the Bogside and beat up some citizens. Later, a man was to die—it was maintained from the treatment which he received during a demonstration. Thus even though Loyalist demonstrators were convicted and imprisoned for their part in these demonstrations (notably the Rev.

Ian Paisley and Major Ronald Bunting for unlawful assembly at Armagh on November 30th, 1968), the Catholic community came to see the R.U.C. as agents of the Protestant community and against all Catholics. The actions of the riot squads in the August 1969 demonstrations merely served to confirm this view, especially as regards the 'B' Specials, a force recruited wholly from Protestants, some of whom were known to have been implicated in the stoning and beating of the People's Democracy march to Derry at Burntollet Bridge in January 1969, and thought to have been implicated also in the Belfast house burning of August 1969.

By barricading off streets in the Falls area in Belfast, and in Bogside and Creggan districts of Derry, the inhabitants constituted 'no-go' areas where the police were not accepted and cut themselves off from the normal protection of law and order. This allowed the thief and looter to act unchecked—except by the activities of the gunmen or para-military power groups in the areas concerned. These 'kangaroo' courts were both spasmodic in operation and frightening in execution. The summary justice meted out, apart from warnings, was to tar and feather the victim and tie him to a lamp standard (on a number of occasions the victim was a female who consorted with a member of the British Army, or who was thought to be giving information). The particular I.R.A. Provisional punishment was to shoot the victim through the knee-cap, with varying degrees of physical damage. Naturally the offence was frequently of a political nature, but also there are known cases of action following certain types of law-breaking activities, a sphere where, compared with the heinous nature of so much perpetrated in their names, extremist organisations of both sides took a very severe view.

A punishment practised by extreme Protestants was to take the victim to a house and there to beat him or her severely. This was ironically called 'rompering', after the name of a local children's television programme. There have been two exceptionally horrifying examples of this——one where a woman was beaten to death whilst her child screamed outside the room, and another where a man was tortured, shot through the mouth and left for dead. He subsequently recovered to some extent and received financial compensation from the State.

The re-organisation of the police force on the recommendation of the Hunt Committee, which included the disbanding of the 'B' Specials and the substitution of an Ulster Defence Regiment under the control of the Army, failed to bring about the desired acceptance of the police in Catholic areas, and the presence of the Army and the escalation of violence made this well-nigh impossible during these years of violence.

When the Army arrived, they did not at first remove the barricades, a fact that was much resented in Protestant areas. The attitude of the first units of the Army was to a large degree typical of a Peace Keeping Force determined not to use violence. There was in fact a criticism that the Army did not interfere enough and incidents are quoted of them standing by seeing acts of vandalism taking place without taking action.

The feeling in Protestant working-class areas was that the British Government, to which they had traditionally given strong allegiance, was giving in to the demands of the 'Fenians', and had stripped

Protestants of the protection of the arms of the R.U.C. and of the 'B' Specials. The substitute, the British Army, they argued, though once invincible, now allowed the Queen's enemies to do what they wanted—enemies whose views appeared to them to be supported by television interviewers. The feeling of insecurity, particularly in the Shankill district, was intensified as they saw their familiar landmarks, and indeed their streets, vanishing to make way for new blocks of flats which, at the bottom of the Shankill Road, were being filled with Catholic families. It was not so paradoxical, therefore, that the area should come into violent confrontation with the Army though in view of the later attitudes of the Catholic community to the Army; it should be noted that the first citizens to be shot by the Army were two Protestants during a Shankill Road riot in October 1969. It is also worth noting that the first R.U.C. man to be killed met his death on the same occasion at the hands of Protestant rioters.

Effects of Internment and Treatment of Political and Violent Offenders

In the face of increasing violence and the impossibility in many cases of finding those willing to risk giving evidence in open court the Stormont Government re-imposed, under the Special Powers Act, internment without trial on 9th August, 1971.

Not only did this spark off a period of intense rioting, but it led also to members of the Catholic community withdrawing their services from public life, such as membership of Boards of Management and Statutory Committees. The measure was regarded by the Catholic community as being

32

aimed exclusively at one section of the population, a belief given credence by the fact that the first 300 'lifted' on 9th August, 1971, were almost all drawn from what could be generally called 'the Catholic community'. In the belief that those likely to be held would be men known to be responsible for the violence a statement was issued in the name of the leaders of the three main Protestant Churches which, with certain provisos, gave guarded support to the measure. It then came to light that many of those interned were those known to have had republican sympathies in the past and that there were also some members of movements like the People's Democracy who had not been connected with violence. These were later released, but the harm had been done.

Further harm was done by the rigorous methods of interrogation used. Reports of 'torture methods' shocked members at Westminster and the former Ombudsman, Sir Edward Compton, was asked to conduct an enquiry. Sir Edward reported in November of that year that there had been no torture or brutality, but admitted 'the following actions that constitute physical ill-treatment: posture on the walls, hooding, noise, deprivation of sleep, diet of bread and water', and added some more individual examples. Documented evidence was published on brutality of Army methods which has not been categorically denied.

Another Commission was set up under Lord Parker 'to consider authorised procedures for the interrogation of persons suspected of terrorism'. This Commission reported in 1972 that those taking part must expect 'discomfort and hardship', but that 'torture whether physical or mental is not justified under any conditions'. Lord Gardiner added a minority report to the effect that to lower standards normally employed in interrogation was not 'morally justifiable and alien to the traditions of what I still believe to be the greatest democracy in the world'.

Cases were brought at the instance of the Irish Government before the European Court of Human Rights. The question of the methods to be used by the State in response to unscrupulous methods employed against it is clearly one of great difficulty, and the findings of the Court have not yet been published. In the case of some men who brought their own cases, the Court in May 1976 rejected their pleas, but on the inconclusive ground that the complainants had not exhausted the legal processes open to them in Northern Ireland.

Subsequently Lord Gardiner acting as Chairman of yet another Commission, this time to examine 'in the light of civil liberties and human rights, measures to deal with terrorism in Northern Ireland'—reported among other suggestions that although his Commission would like to see the end of detention without trial, 'the present level of increased violence, and the difficulty of predicting events even a few months ahead, make it impossible to put forward a precise recommendation on the timing'.

The Secretary of State, Mr. Rees, announced, after the Provisional I.R.A. had called a cease-fire, that it was his intention to release all men held without trial by the end of 1975, unless the level of violence made this in his opinion impossible. The Loyalist internees (numbering about 60 at the highest point) were released by the middle of the year, and by December 1975, the last Republican internee was also freed.

Both internment and the imprisonment following conviction of greatly increased numbers have imposed strains on an increased number of families, of parents, wives and children. In the first instance, relations found it difficult to find out just what had happened to those who had been arrested and then visits that they naturally desired to make to the Maze (and later Magilligan) prison proved both costly and time-consuming. There seemed to be a social pressure to take a large amount of extra food and any 'comforts' allowed, although adequate (if not always well-served) food was provided. Support for the families of those interned at first was augmented by strong political and emotional over-tones and funds flowed in from the U.S.A. and from local sources. An agreement was made with the Supplementary Benefits Commission to 'disregard' as regular family income £3 a week, to be used for travel on prison visiting and extra supplies, but loss of earnings brought hardship to many families.

The violence led to a new category of prisoner—the political or special category which carried with it privileges over numbers of visits, the wearing of private clothing, etc., which are denied to the ordinary prisoner. The Gardiner Committee recom-mended that this category be done away with, but it is recognised that this is difficult while prisoners remain with these privileges. The Secretary of State, however, announced in December 1975 that no men charged after March 1976 would be admitted to the status of special category prisoners.

Fewer were interned on the Loyalist side where it was somewhat easier to secure convictions in the courts. In large measure this was because the R.U.C. was not operating in Republican areas where, for the most part, the Army made the arrests. The Army are not trained in the securing of legal convictions as are the police, quite apart from the difficulty of finding those who would give evidence in court.

Political and Sectarian Assassinations

A particularly unsavoury feature of the civil disturbances has been the deliberate assassination of individuals. This has taken two forms: the killing of members of the opposite community, whether by way of revenge or of elimination of unwanted elements from an area; and the killing—often described as 'execution'—of members of the same community, whether on account of differences of policy or of alleged treachery and informing. Feuds between para-military groups within each community have resulted in a considerable number of deaths. The Official I.R.A., committed to a Marxist approach, professed to hope to exert the kind of political pressure which would eventually win over Protestant workers to a 32-county workers' Republic of Ireland. The Provisionals broke away in order to assert the permanent objective of expelling the British and would claim that the victims of their assassinations were 'military targets': policemen, soldiers, members of the judiciary, etc. They state that they do not wish to kill Irishmen—though some, they admit, will inevitably get killed in the course of a campaign to free their country. This can only seem a sophistry to those who have experienced the results of their campaign. The plain fact is that hundreds of Irishmen are dead as the direct result of Provisional actions.

Loyalists, on the other hand, have little means of identifying the particular members of the other community against whom their revenge should be directed. In consequence they often seem, whether this is really the case or not, to be killing Catholics just because they are Catholics. The upsurge of this kind of activity on their part early in 1975 helped to restore support to the Provisionals at a time when their 'cease-fire' revealed a sense of weakness.

Internecine murders on both sides have often appeared to follow a decision by some kind of kangaroo court. The victims have been 'condemned to death' and shortly afterwards shot. In other cases known members of a rival organisation — I.R.S.P. as against Official I.R.A.—U.V.F. against U.D.A.—have been shot at sight, in the streets or in their homes during periods of open feud.

To the ordinary law-abiding citizen these horrifying events are seen as ruthless murder and the local press has long since exhausted the vocabulary of horror in describing them. They should be seen, however, as the inevitable concomitants of a lawless situation in which large sections of the population are prepared to condone the use of force by their own side while crying havoc at the results of its use by the other side.

Republicans see their campaign in military terms, a liberation of their country from oppression. Much Loyalist action is the result of the frustration of seeing the Army unable to end Republican violence. The result is continuous loss of life and the further polarisation of communities destined to share one country.

The Ulster Workers' Council Strike

No account of the incidence of violence would be complete without a note of the Ulster Workers' Council strike in May 1974, when after 14 days of strike action the power-sharing Executive of the Northern Ireland Assembly (set up following the 1973 Sunningdale Agreement) resigned, to be followed by another period of direct Westminster rule.

In the course of a few days a virtual stranglehold of the industrial life of the country was established. This paralysed the central government in a way which the I.R.A. with all their violent means had not been able to achieve. During this period there was a remarkable diminution of overt violence while the Provisionals watched, presumably, to see the Loyalists wreck their own land. The Army watched, too, permitting widespread illegality in its very presence. Perhaps the standing threat to sabotage the power stations was the basic reason for this.

Following an emotional meeting in Ballymena, a Protestant gang entered a public house and killed two Catholics; some petrol stations which refused to close down were wrecked; and dire threats were issued by various Protestant para-military groups against anyone breaking the strike. These facts show how far this action was from being an example of pure non-violence in action. The threat of violence was implicit throughout—on the other hand Protestant support from the start was by no means generally due to intimidation. There was certainly a misreading of the extent of this support by the Northern Ireland Office and by the Northern Committee of I.C.T.U. The march 'back to work' organised by the latter, with support from the British T.U.C., was a failure. Indeed clumsy and uncertain government handling of the stoppage increased popular support. The Prime Minister's broadcast with its reference to 'spongers' exacerbated the situation. The effects of these mistakes are still with us.

The U.W.C., with man and brain power supplied by the Vanguard Party, organised the delivery of essential supplies for hospitals, children's and old people's homes. Their leaders made much of this, and Mr. Rees hesitated to bring in the Army to take control (which would have been a massive and very complicated task). Had the Executive not resigned when it did, resulting in the calling off of the strike at once, then there would have been suffering in many quarters, certainly in Catholic areas, where businesses did not close down, but where replenishing of supplies through a Loyalists' boycott would have been well nigh impossible. The picketing of roads and menacing at some points nevertheless occurred without actual acts of violence, although the threat was always there.

Ostensibly directed against the idea of a Council of Ireland the strike was an emotional reaction to the whole Sunningdale policy. It was tragic in that the power-sharing Executive, to which it put an end, had made a good start and was showing initiative. Perhaps it could have been avoided if more attention had been paid to the significance of the Northern Ireland voting in the U.K. elections of February.

The Churchmen's Initiative and the Cease-Fire

Towards the end of 1974, contact was made with the Provisional Wing of the I.R.A. by some Protestant churchmen acting on their own initiative. A meeting was arranged on December 9th to 11th of that year at Feakle, Co. Clare, in the Republic of Ireland, between a number of Provisional leaders and an *ad hoc* group of leading Irish churchmen reinforced by two from Britain. The outcome was that the Provisionals agreed to a cease-fire to last over Christmas. Coinciding with the Call to Peace issued by the official Church leaders (see p. 68), this caused a revival of hope in the community. At this stage the Churchmen contacted the Secretary of State, Mr. Merlyn Rees, and the Northern Ireland Office carried out negotiations with the Sinn Fein Party, the political wing of the Provisionals. The cease-fire was extended after Christmas, and on February 10th it was agreed that it should be extended indefinitely. The Provisionals agreed to set up a number of 'Incident Centres' which would investigate and report to the Northern Ireland Office on any alleged breaches.

As far as the bombing and overt Provisional activity was concerned this cease-fire, although at no time complete and without incident, brought much needed relief to the Province, especially in Belfast and Londonderry and other provincial towns. People began to move about with a greater feeling of security, and cultural, sporting and, above all, evening activities gained more support.

The cease-fire did not mean, alas, the end of violence. Whatever may have been the intentions of the Provisionals, the incidence after a few weeks of murders of Catholics made it difficult for them to avoid some degree of activity, although the excuse given was more often harassment by the Army. Gradually the number of incidents of violence increased, particularly in the South Armagh area, where the hilly terrain gave good cover for gunmen to attack members of the security forces, and where the Protestant population in the minority felt threatened. It appeared that the Provisionals operating in this area were acting at times autonomously. Arrests in the Republic had the effect of changing the composition of the Provisional Army Council. Towards the end of the year the term cease-fire became a mockery, and eventually the incident centres were closed down. A new threat of violence was issued early in 1976 by the Provisional I.R.A. which was followed by a number of revenge murders of greater intensity than witnessed to date since the current disturbances began.

The story of these years and, perhaps of 1975 in particular, serves to underline an obvious truth: that once violence breaks out it is extremely difficult to stop it. A grave question exists whether the organisers of it can effectively 'call off' their men. Irregulars exist on all sides who do not acknowledge the leadership. Criminal elements, with no cause to serve but their own warped satisfaction, flourish when the police are overstretched and some forms of violence are condoned. Young people grow up in an atmosphere where violent solutions to problems are taken for granted. Even with a more unequivocal support from all sections of the community, the forces of law and order are confronted with a well nigh impossible task in sorting out the variously motivated groups and in taking action without alienating some of those not yet engaged in violence. Furthermore the violence that begins in one state, ostensibly the one in which grievance and injustice are present, inevitably spreads to others, as bomb incidents in Dublin, Dundalk and Birmingham bear witness.

2. The Results of Violence

The Political Efficacy of Violence

We saw above (p. 22) that the aims of the Civil Rights' Movement were to a great extent realised and that this was done without resort to violence. We may now ask how far violence by the Republican Movement since 1969 has achieved the stated objects of the movement which may be summarised as :

(a) to achieve the downfall of the Stormont Parliament and the end of the Unionist monopoly of government;

(b) to drive the British out of Northern Ireland;

(c) to achieve, in one form or another, a united Ireland.

To take these in reverse order, it is clear that (c) has not been realised. It would probably be widely agreed that the events of 1968-76 have removed any possibility that might earlier have existed of the re-unification of Ireland in the foreseeable future. Indeed the ineptitude of the Provisionals' campaign is underlined by the way in which many in the Republic who in the '60's set their sights on the early achievement of Irish unity are now convinced that it can only come about in the distant future.

It is equally clear that (b) has not been achieved, though some would say that substantial progress towards it has been made, whether by weakening the British will to remain or by provoking a movement for independence for Northern Ireland. Thus we are left with the first aim, the dismantling of Stormont. This has occurred and the question for consideration is the extent to which that event is attributable to Republican violence.

On March 10th, 1972, the Provisional I.R.A. called a 72-hour truce and listed three conditions for the continuance of inactivity beyond that limit. They were: withdrawal of British forces, total amnesty for political prisoners, and the abolition of Stormont. On March 24th the Stormont Parliament was prorogued and direct rule instituted. That kind of conjunction of events is all too easily seen as a concessionary response to a demand. It was, of course, nothing of the kind. No purpose would have been served by giving way completely on one point of a three point ultimatum and doing nothing at all about the other two points.

So long as the internal discussions at cabinet level, in Stormont and in Westminster, remain confidential, it will be impossible to be definitive about the motivation of the British government in suspending Stormont. The first point to emphasise, however, is that the British government did it. It was not achieved directly by any action in Northern Ireland, but was a considered step by the British government in pursuance of a policy to deal with the situation. On the other hand it is equally clear that the British government would have been very unlikely so to act except in conditions of extreme crisis, and it had been sustained violence that had brought about those conditions.

The following factors in the situation then obtaining are significant :

Ever since the Army had been called in (summer 1969) control of security had been difficult and anomalous, in that responsibility for public order rested with the Minister of Home Affairs and the cabinet at Stormont, while the Army was controlled by the Secretary of State for Defence and the cabinet in Whitehall. As the situation grew more grave this divided control became more dangerous. The events of 'Bloody Sunday' in January 1972 undoubtedly helped to bring home to the British government how extremely grave the situation had become. The divided control could not possibly be resolved by putting the Army under the direction of a provincial government; and so it could only be resolved by transferring the responsibility for law and order to Westminster. Rightly or wrongly the Stormont government resisted this. If London took law and order, London must take everything.

The introduction of internment in August 1971 was the responsibility of the Stormont government. It was taken on the personal initiative of Mr. Faulkner. Its effect had been to unite the minority population as never before. The earlier withdrawal of the S.D.L.P. from Parliament, the civil disobedience campaign (rent and rates strike) and the 'alternative assembly': all these non-violent initiatives were so intensified as to render virtually impossible any political initiative to solve the problem of governing Northern Ireland. Westminster recognised this and was insisting in March 1972 that a start be made with phasing out internment. There is no doubt that Mr. Whitelaw hoped to do this and he did in fact go a long way in releasing internees during the early months of his period as Secretary of State.

For these reasons it is fair to say that direct rule was a step taken by the British government deliberately to create conditions in which progress towards a political solution could be made. It was not a weak concession to Republican violence but a strong confrontation of Loyalist attitudes. At the same time it would not have been necessary without the campaign of violence that provoked internment and all its consequences; and to that extent it was indirectly brought about by Republican violence.

It can thus be shown that the main objectives of Republican policy have not been achieved by violence or the threat of it. If certain secondary objectives have, on both sides, been so achieved, it remains true that these achievements have not contributed to the realisation of long-term purposes.

Physical and Economic Effects of Violence

The physical effects of violence are only too apparent in terms of the maimed and crippled bodies, the blighted lives and the appalling and wanton destruction of property; they need not be dwelt upon further at this point.

The economic effects are both direct and indirect with the latter being especially difficult to determine. Since 1968 to the end of February 1976 there have been almost 25,900 claims for injuries to persons. Some 16,000 of these have been dealt with leaving almost 10,000 still outstanding. The amount paid in compensation for the 16,000 claims was over £20 million. Claims for damage to property numbered over 105,000 for the same period. Of these, more than 81,000 have been dealt with and about 24,000 are outstanding. The total compensation paid on the 81,000 claims was over £140 million. The total payments made have amounted to £160 million and clearly those still outstanding will almost certainly bring the figure well over £200 million.

Stated baldly like this, these figures may seem abstract and unreal but they have, in fact, a terrifying reality. The total number of personal injury claims represents one person out of every 60 for the whole population of Northern Ireland and clearly a higher proportion still for Belfast and Derry, where most of the injuries will have taken place. The sum of £160 million paid out in compensation is actually some £20 million more than was spent on the whole health service in Northern Ireland during 1974-75. Alternatively if the people of Northern Ireland had to meet from their own resources the cost of personal injury and property damage claims they would almost certainly have to cut drastically the standard of services they now enjoy. This prompts the further question whether or not we have been seriously over-protected from the consequences of our own violence. Can anyone doubt that if we had to pay the full economic cost of our own violence we would not have condoned it to the extent that we have ?

But as indicated earlier the full economic cost is difficult to determine. It includes not only the millions referred to above, but the lost economic activity that goes with physical damage to and destruction of persons and property, both the direct and indirect losses. The latter would include some part of the earnings which the tourist industry would have made, as well as the losses that are already apparent and in store for the future because of the fall off in investment which would otherwise have taken place. This will be seen in the future in terms of lower incomes, higher unemployment and greater emigration than would otherwise have arisen. Then there are the additional security costs which the violence has made necessary; these too, even after allowing for various offsets, would run into tens of millions of pounds.

The Psychological, Moral and Social Effects of Violence

The experience of living in riot areas during prolonged periods of fear and tension cannot have left the nervous systems of the population untouched and one would presume that there would be an effect also on the minds and personalities of the citizens.

It came as a surprise to many to learn after the first year or two of rioting that (as in fact in times of national war) there had been an appreciable drop in the suicide rate. On the other hand, numerous studies have been published, particularly by Dr. H. A. Lyons and Dr. Morris Fraser showing where the strain of riot conditions has led to mental breakdown in adults and in children. There is general agreement on the great increase in the use of sedatives since the advent of civil disturbances and all connected with any form of social work, certainly in Belfast, will report that the phrase 'she's been bad with her nerves since the troubles' is an oft repeated cliche.

As against this, Dr. Lyons notes that where rival sectarian groups attack each other, or attack the Army, 'there has been a drop in the taking of drugs among teenagers in the troubled areas, although this drop might partly be due to the fact that the illegal organisations controlling these areas discourage forcefully anyone pushing drugs'.

But by far the most obvious effect of widespread political violence is that — by definition — it constitutes a break-down of law and order. We should by now in Ireland be aware of just what this means in terms of death, maiming, intimidation and destruction of property. Justice, as ordinarily understood, disappears for many; and the most basic of human rights — the right to live — is aborted; inhumanity, hate and fear are the fruits of such violence.

With the general disorder consequent upon the use of violence has gone a serious deterioration in moral standards. There has been a catastrophic and terrifying decline in respect for the sacredness of human life. Consciences have become callous in respect of murder, torture, maiming; and needless to say also of destruction of property and injuries to persons. The political 'cause' has been thought to justify without question all sorts of crimes and immorality. For the sake of the 'cause' robbery has become commonplace. Extortion, threats and intimidation have been used by para-military bodies and their supporters for the collection of funds. Various kinds of thinly veiled extortion rackets have gone on under the cover of political violence.

A concomitant of political violence has been a great increase in plain vandalism, theft and crime. Oppression and harassment have taken on new meanings, being now the fate of whole communities at the mercy of their para-military so-called protectors. The recruitment of young people into the para-military movements and the systematic indoctrination of teenagers in the practice and philosophy of violence are particularly frightening for the future. There has been a disastrous increase in excessive drinking, particularly among teenagers and sometimes even children. There are disturbing signs also of a breakdown in standards of sexual morality. Marital infidelity, in particular, seems to be on the increase. Indeed, the sanctity of marriage and the unity and peace of the family and the home are particularly threatened in conditions of violence.

The evil fruits of violence would in themselves be enough to show its intrinsic evil in the Irish situation. It may take generations before the terrible moral and spiritual price for these years of violence is paid. The sanctity of human life, which is a central Gospel principle as well as a basic human value, has been seriously eroded. The consequences for the future of Christian society in Ireland, indeed for the future of ordinary civilised living, are grave indeed. No conceivable political result could justify it. Irish experience could well stand as a conclusive demonstration of both the evil and the ineffectiveness of violence as a means to desirable social change.

But there are still other effects of political violence which are at least as important and perhaps are more insidious, especially in a society as divided as ours. Historically, political violence and the threat of it in Ireland has been honoured and romanticised—the Ulster Volunteers of 1912 and the men of the 1916 rising are now heroes. But surely the savagery that we have experienced since 1969 and the corruption of civilised thought and feeling demands a radical re-appraisal by all Irishmen of the romantic view of resort to physical force which we have inherited from those years.

Furthermore, the question must be faced whether or not the mass of the people in our society condone, perhaps partly out of fear of reprisals, political violence, if not actively then passively. To put the matter differently — why is there not an overwhelming demand for the support of the police and other security forces in Northern Ireland and a determination on the part of individuals, groups and institutions to do everything possible to re-establish civilised processes of law and order ? Is it because of fear of violence or because of thoughts and feelings, both political and other, which existed before recent violence had polarised our chronically divided community ? Here effect and cause become inextricable in a vicious circle of tragedy. Is the political violence itself a consequence of, or a continuing cause of, the underlying divisions of the community ? What weight must be given to the feeling on the part of many that a State which was established against the will of a third of its population cannot claim their whole-hearted allegiance ? Or on the other hand to the feeling that the will of the majority must prevail even if that involves harsh measures of control which those who do not share the feeling will call in question? But if the efficacy of 'majority rule' depends, in Western democracies on a voluntary consensus of the whole people or society, then how far is the lack of consensus, indeed the deep division of allegiance, to be equated with a religious division — a division between Catholic and Protestants? How far are the terrorists of both sides 'extensions of us', in the sense that we have made do with an uneasy co-existence where we should have sought long since a positive reconciliation? Is terrorism a rejection of the ethos of our society? Or is it, as some of us would regretfully think, a manifestation of that ethos?

The vocation of the Churches in such a situation is something that we must leave for detailed treatment in the last chapter. Here we simply point out that acute questions are raised about the relationship of individuals and institutions to the political structure of society. One of the effects of violence is, indeed, to confront the Churches in an inescapable way with the Church - State problem that remains latent in easier times. To call for the establishment of peace and for the full restoration of the processes of law and order seem to some synonymous with the support of the existing state; to others it does not. Can the Churches specify what or whose peace they seek and spell out a concrete programme where the best efforts of well-intentioned politicians have failed ? Or must they confine themselves to appeals whose vague character reflects a basic neutrality on—or even an evasion of—the concrete issues ? Is the price of precision a re-opening of the divide, as each Church adopts the programme its members favour ? The Churches are called neither to exhortation nor to neutrality but to a positive ministry of reconciliation, costly perhaps and radical in relation to some inherited stances, and entailing active support for proposals which seem to afford a real prospect of a just, peaceful and lasting solution.

The Effects of Violence on Children and Young People

In considering the effects of the current violence upon young people growing up in Northern Ireland one must not overlook the general alienation of youth in all parts of the world that characterised the '60's. It was not only here that the authority of parents and schools was called sharply in question and that 'the generation gap' became a popular phrase. Young people began to have much more spending money than in earlier generations; alcohol and drugs were more freely available to them; sexual permissiveness led to new forms of semi-permanent group relationships in which both sexes were involved; ease of transport made it common-place for boys and girls to run away from home, and fear that they might do so often inhibited parents from the exercise of discipline. All these tendencies were present in our society before the 'troubles' began. If on the one hand, young people in Northern Ireland were a little behind the times in their adoption of these attitudes, the compara-tively under-privileged conditions in which much of the youth of Belfast lived contributed to the irresponsibility that characterised some elements. Truancy, vandalism, and petty crime were by no means unknown before 1969.

All these phenomena were, however, sharply exacerbated by the outbreak of civil unrest. To find that the growing boys' combative fantasies—'Cow-boys and Indians', 'Cops and Robbers'—are actually being enacted by their seniors in real life in their own streets is to be caught up into a world where any moral restraint on violent conduct is unlikely to have much effect. To this has to be added the glamour and publicity accorded by the media to the activities of the young.

Children have been known to be asked to pose in various militaristic games postures. Children of ten or eleven have been put in possession of lethal weapons by people wishing to render well-nigh impossible the activities of the security forces. Stories that young children have used their position in illegal or extremist organisations to threaten their teachers in school have been largely discounted, but it is a fact that teenagers have played a role, at least as catalysts, in the transition from Civil Rights demonstrations to violent street conflict, first against rival gangs and then in organised terrorist activity. Stone-throwing by young people against the Army was 'taken over' by the Provisional wing of the I.R.A., while the consequent notoriety and glory was soon a stimulus to Protestant youth in the formation of Tartan Gangs to beat up young Catholics. On both sides these youngsters were recruited early in the respective para-military units.

A play group organiser in Belfast writes :

'It is unnerving to think of the consequences in terms of self-image and self-esteem that the street fighting is having on the Irish boys and girls so involved. To see themselves on television, to know that they are making world headlines, to feel themselves shaping history, to sing songs that immortalise their names . . .'

All this was at a certain stage a potent factor in the mentality of many young people especially in Belfast. A headmaster summed up as follows the main effects of violence, as he saw them :

(a) A fair proportion of youth have become affiliated in one way or another with para-military organisations or gangs and have access to lethal firearms.

(b) Young people are being lured into social clubs where they partake of liquor and, possibly, other pleasurable attractions.

(c) Many of the normal restraints which prevent people from theft or injury to a neighbour's property do not exist.

(d) Young people are being used by adult leaders to create mob scenes and to swell the ranks of their parades.

53

(e) Young people of today have been reared in a violent environment and know no other.

(f) Violence has intensified as it has continued and it feeds — and is fed — on the FEARS of Roman Catholics and Protestants alike.

(g) There has been a marked drop in school attendance since the violence began: in some areas from over 90% to around 75%. This will have very serious consequences.

Yet in spite of that gloomy catalogue the schools —in both communities—have played a notable part in sustaining educational standards and in providing an oasis of normality in the life of many young people. Examination results have shown no decline. A teacher in a Catholic school writes :

'It is a stringent rule of school that no pupil or member of staff is allowed to further his particular views when he comes through the school gates. The school is therefore politically neutral ... The pupils do not confuse the authority of the school with the authority of the "forces of law and order". Even after full scale riots the pupils come back to school and submit to school discipline without demur. This is because we have always insisted on a code of justice in school.'

Fluctuating enrolments and staff recruitment has made for major difficulties in some areas but

'for many children their schools have provided a stable environment at a time when the other formative medio —television, newspapers, the gable walls, oral communications—are depicting chaos'.

This teacher also affirms that when Catholics are treated as first class citizens there will be a bright future for all.

A hopeful feature is that where young folk have gone off on a mixed holiday camp, all have got on well, by and large, together. It is difficult to bring such groups together again once they have returned to their own segregated living areas. Nevertheless some progress has been made in this and in one of the notoriously troubled areas of Belfast. Protestant and Catholic schools share a common centre in the country for rural pursuits.

By and large, youth is very resilient and although the violence may have upset some children so that they cannot any longer cope with life, these are few. The future presents two major problems—how to put a challenging activity in place of the excitement and destruction of violence; and how to integrate a community where, for many, the other side has come to be regarded as, literally and physically, 'the enemy'. Our headmaster informant had the following suggestions to make :

(a) Awaken the political consciousness of the people . . . to the fact that their basic problems are similar.

(b) Disestablishment of the 'Clerical Church' from education and from formal involvement in the Orange Order.

(c) Church must be orientated more towards the ordinary working people.

(d) Education should take on a much greater social dimension.

(e) Youth organisations . . . must be attractive not only to the 'good boys'.

(f) Sunday schools need to be re-examined. Good will and obsolete theology, with poor pedagogy, are not good enough today.

(g) The confidence of youth and social leadership must be restored.

(h) The training of teachers should be integrated.

The Working Party reports the foregoing ideas and opinions without comment and without necessarily committing its members to all or any of them. The purpose of this section will have been fulfilled if readers recognise the disastrous consequences wreaked upon the moral and spiritual development of a new generation by the violence that its elders have perpetuated or condoned.

3. The Teaching of the Churches

It is easy to jump to conclusions about what the teaching of the Churches ought to be in a situation of conflict. 'Christian love demands non-violence in all circumstances'; 'Christian obedience requires support at all times for the powers that be'; 'The moral failings of "the other side", whether infidel, heretic, or modern communist, justify a crusade': all these simplistic views are in some quarters embraced with enthusiasm and upheld with tenacity. But the dilemmas are profound. Before attempting to elucidate the task of the Churches in Ireland today we have therefore considered it right to devote attention to the general problems that arise when the teaching of Christianity is applied to the issues of the State, of war and revolution.

The Christian and the State

The foundation of a Christian view of the state has been traditionally found in Paul's letter to the Romans Chapter 13:1-7 where it seems to be said quite unambiguously that the state has been instituted by God, with the function of repressing evil and encouraging good. From this basic starting point, the duties of the Christian to the state can be quickly spelled out; the Christian will pray for the state, its people and its government; he will be a loyal and obedient subject, co-operating with the state in promoting the welfare of the citizens and of lending moral support to the state when it upholds good and represses evil; he will see as part of his responsibility the necessary criticism of the state when it departs from these ends and will seek to recall men to the standards of justice and principles of conduct set forth in the Word of God; he will seek to permeate public life with the spirit of Christ and participate in it to this end.

It is clear that this allegiance of the Christian to the state is no unthinking, uncritical, blind loyalty. It was to people in authority that the apostles said 'We ought to obey God rather than men'; but that does not necessarily mean 'obey men who represent God rather than other men'! It would have been easier for us if Jesus had made a distinction between 'the things that are Caesar's and the things that are Caiaphas's'. For if both State and Church are instruments of God's will in their respective spheres, then all things are God's, and if God declares what is Caesar's, it is also God who declares the sphere of ecclesiastical authority. Both are exercised by human agents and both have been known to exceed their sphere. There is no part of his life for the Christian in which Jesus Christ is not Lord. The Christian's obedience to the State is a matter of conscience and limited by conscience, in the sense that it must not involve disobedience to the will of God as his informed conscience apprehends it.

Furthermore the teaching of Paul on obedience was addressed to people living under an autocracy. The transition to democratic institutions means that a duty lies on the Christian not simply to acknowledge authority and support it, but also to play a part in determining the course that the State will pursue. In particular the transition has brought about a situation in which government is not stable unless it is based on a general consensus of the governed. To secure that consensus and to build upon it a just structure with morally sound aims is the function of a Christian statesman. Mere assertion of authority, whether based on force or on a claim to obedience, will no longer serve.

The Christian is a realist. He recognises that the state through its sinful misuse of power, effected often through its monopoly of the means of coercion, becomes often an instrument of evil. There is indeed a strong strand of biblical teaching which sees secular government as demonically controlled, a view that finds clear expression in Revelation Chapter 13. The contrast of this outlook with that of Paul outlined above, is probably to be explained by the fact that Romans 13 was written before and Revelation 13 after the initiation of the persecution of Christians by the Roman state. How is the Christian to act in such a situation ? Is he to be guided by examples of revolutionary involvement in political change and upheaval that he reads of in the Old Testament ? Or does the life and teaching of Jesus and his living lordship of life dictate a radically different stance ?

The Christian and War

No answer to these questions can be found without first considering the almost insoluble moral problem with which the practice of war has confronted the Christian conscience from New Testament times. Let us first state the case for Christian action to be based on the total rejection of physical force. There have been through the centuries Christians who have called for a total renunciation of war and killing on any basis, for total commitment to the principle of pacifism, asserting the demand that the Christian lose his or her life rather than wilfully destroy the life of another, even an aggressor. At times this pacifism may be related to a world-renouncing ethic, typified either by complete withdrawal from the 'evil' world to the secluded isolation of the monastery, or by complete withdrawal from socio-political concern into a world of pietistic concentration on the 'soul' whilst living in the world. But there is an 'active' pacifism which though totally committed to non-violence, is yet actively involved in the imperfect and at times evil world, for the promotion of the common good and the redress of established wrong. Such pacifists are dedicated to the 'maximal' use of non-violent means (be they constitutional or unconstitutional) in the pursuit of virtuous social goals. Although, the active pacifist believes in the ultimate efficacy and efficiency of non-violent means, he or she is prepared to suffer apparent defeat or injury in the short term, rather than resort to violence.

The position of the active pacifist is clear : The Christian is committed to the pursuit of virtuous social goals by exclusively moral means but violence is immoral and therefore the Christian may never use violence as a means in the pursuit of any goal. He believes that this is not only logical but is an authentic expression of the stance of Jesus, as when he said that we were to 'love our enemies, do good to those who hate us; bless those who curse us and pray for those who maltreat us' and 'to do to others what we would have them do to us'.

This position raises acute difficulties in practice. What if the non-violence precipitates a violent response ? Does not the non-violence then itself become in some sense a cause of violence and to that extent a contradiction ? Does loving our enemies necessarily mean abstaining from resistance to evil designs that they may have ? And so the Christian Church as a whole, at any rate since the time when the Church became officially accepted by the state, has felt compelled to take a different view. Those who adopt this view argue for a necessary distinction to be made between force and violence. Force may be defined in this context as pressure, physical or moral, used to resolve conflict. It is the unlawful use of force which is violence. All states have to use force for the restraint of anti-social elements. Such force becomes unlawful, when it is exercised by those who have no right to exercise it (e.g. when a man murders a fellow man) or when the mode or degree of force used is excessive (e.g. police action in a totalitarian regime). When the state uses its coercive powers in the interests of justice and in the pursuit of law and order, the Christian has then, it is believed, a moral obligation to support and participate in the state's legal killing, though many question the morality of capital punishment in our time. But though the authorities are ordained by God, they remain sinful men who are prone to act for ends other than those to which they have been appointed and as a consequence it is the duty of Christians to scrutinise carefully the ends for which the state uses its power and the way in which force is exercised. There is here no attempt to 'justify' every war or every exercise of power by a state. The concept of the 'just war' as it has been refined in the experience of the Church, provides, it is believed by many, a general test of the legitimacy of the ultimate force of war, perhaps also of revolution. A recent consideration of this concept lists the following six conditions that need to be met to 'justify' Christian involvement in such activity :

a. there must a just cause

b. force must be the only way left of effecting change

c. there must be a properly constituted authority to direct the action

d. there must be a feasible goal

e. the means must be appropriate to the end

f. reconciliation must be sought as the ultimate end.

There has always been great difficulty about the practical application of these tests and many theologians have found them to be in danger of obsolescence when weapons of mass destruction have changed the character of warfare. Even where a conflict on a lesser scale occurs, one may ask such questions as whether 'the only way of effecting change' means 'the only way of getting it *now*' or whether one should be prepared to wait for a long term historical solution to emerge. Those who argue for the continuing relevance of the concept of the 'just war' do not seek to argue that the practice of warfare is other than evil. They would agree with the historian Gibbon that 'war in its fairest form implies a perpetual violation of humanity and justice'. But they would argue that the refusal to be involved in war would at times be to participate in the perpetuation of even greater evil.

The Christian and Revolution

We cannot hope here to provide any neat formula to harmonise these distinctive positions held passionately by Christians. We ourselves are divided in our understanding of the Christian obligation in these matters, but not on denominational lines: there were pacifists and non-pacifists in both the Catholic and Protestant membership of the working party. Yet it is in the context of this division in Christian testimony that we must review the question of the Christian and revolution.

And we must first listen to those who argue for total Christian commitment to non-violence against the state because the Christian is called to be revolutionary according to the pattern of Jesus, according to non-violence. The ethic of Jesus must surely be normative for all Christians. The Christian is to have the mind which was in Christ Jesus, he is to be 'conformed to the image' of Christ, and abiding in Christ he is to 'walk in the same way in which he walked'. It is highly significant that in a politically explosive situation, confronted by the way of violent insurrection in the Zealot movement's protest against the imperial Roman power, Jesus rejected such a way. He neither used violence on behalf of the weak, the poor, the suffering with whom he so closely identified, nor in his own defence; but rather he submitted himself to the authorities, even to death. His way was the way of the cross, that cross which becomes the central symbol in the Christian understanding of God's method of dealing with evil. What could be more revolutionary than this method of overcoming evil with good, this challenge to man's seemingly incorrigible reliance upon violent ways, man's seemingly incurable arrogance in claiming for himself the right to kill and to torture ?

The strength of this case cannot be denied. Attempts to challenge it by portraying Jesus as a guerilla type revolutionary, have failed pathetically. And yet there is a case to be made for the possibility of what we may call a 'just rebellion'. Those who hold to this view note that Jesus met with and talked with soldiers, yet never did he apply to their profession the prohibition of the commandment against killing. But the ground for holding to the possibility of a 'just rebellion' rests on the basis that the power of rulers is a trust from God to be exercised for the common good. If a government utterly fails to fulfil its God-given function, or lacks, because it was intruded by aliens or has governed tyrannically, the consent of most of those governed, authority lapses back to God who may then call new rulers into being. And as war cannot be waged except as a last resort and by means appropriate to the ends, so rebellion must fulfil like conditions if it to be 'justified'. There are even here violent methods of struggle in which Christians must not participate, such as, for example, torture, in any form, the holding of innocent hostages, the deliberate or indiscriminate killing of innocent noncombatants.

How are we to evaluate these two positions ?

If to hope for a violent rebellion that does not involve the use of reprehensible methods of conflict is a naive hope in the light of all experience of rebellion, and particularly our own experience here in Ireland, then a serious question mark is posed against the possibility of a 'just rebellion'. If we cannot agree on a policy of absolute pacifism, yet we are compelled to a pragmatic rejection of violence, on the grounds that it has such tragic consequences that it can rarely if ever be balanced by any commensurate good. If the Christian, in the light of this and in seeking to conform his life to the life style of his Lord, must be profoundly uneasy about any involvement in violence, it must follow that he has a right to promote the way of non-violence; but only if he is committed to the total life style of Jesus, in his radical identification in loving concern with the poor, the weak, the suffering, is this witness authentically Christian. We must now attempt to spell out some of the implications we see in this. In this chapter we do so in general terms and in the next we seek to make direct application to the problems of Ireland.

Some practical implications

a. If as Christians we are deeply disturbed by the increase of violence throughout the world we have to acknowledge a large share of the responsibility. We have not lived up to the word of our Lord that we are to be 'the salt of the earth and the light of the world'; we must therefore repent before God and awaken in all Christians the spirit of repentance for things done and left undone; and we must resolve by God's grace to do our utmost to prevent the repetition of such sins in the future.

b. Christians must be actively involved in the pursuit of a just society, and to that end be the creators of viable non-violent means of redressing social wrong and promoting social good. In this context we must not shun the call to a prophetic denunciation of injustice nor to demonstrate our solidarity with the poor and deprived. We must be

64

willing to see the total removal of the Churches from positions of privilege in society. There must be more simplicity, more participation and sharing of responsibility within the Church structures to provide a model for society.

c. Christians must play their full part in political life, so that the spirit of the Gospel can inspire and shape political life and social institutions. Only a few will take a leading part in public affairs; but it is important that those who have the talent and feel the challenge of this should not withdraw because of the arduous and often distasteful nature of public life. All Christians have the duty to exercise the franchise in a thoughtful and responsible way, not necessarily 'going with the wind'; and all have a duty, in greater or less measure, to influence public opinion by their sober and charitable expression of views on public questions.

d. Christians must seek reconciliation between parties separated by barriers of injustice or by traditionally hostile attitudes. Reconciliation begins with a sincere and patient effort to understand as fully as possible the case for the opponent's point of view. It continues with an honest attempt to weigh that case against one's own and to see where justice lies. It proceeds to a resolute search for common ground or for means to remedy grievances without creating counter injustice. It culminates in a willingness to repent of past wrongs, to make costly overtures and to run major risks, whether of rebuff or treachery. It is inspired throughout, not simply by a desire to put an end to a difficult situation, but by a positive and God-given will to establish relationships of love and charity with all men.

e. There must be among Christians a genuine open pursuit of unity despite all the difficulties that lie in the way. This pursuit must not remain at the level of discussions at the 'top', welcome though these are, but reach to the parishes and congregations. Here imaginative steps need to be taken to promote the awareness of the bonds which unite divided Christians in Christ, and co-operation between divided Christians in social and charitable works on a growing scale should be encouraged.

f. Christians must discourage to the best of their ability the glorification of violence in war and revolution. The martial virtues of courage, fortitude and self-sacrifice rightly evoke respect and admiration and have been displayed by many who took part in war with reluctance and misgiving. Yet they can easily be exploited to disguise the evil nature of warfare and are sometimes confused with aggression and ferocity. Their existence does not in itself render good the cause in which they are displayed.

g. Christians must above all engage in the task of proclaiming the Gospel in word and deed in a renewed effort to open men's hearts to the grace and truth of Christ, for only from this source can come forgiveness, patience, peace and reconciliation; only in Christ do we see that violence is an assault upon a brother made in the image of his God and redeemed by Christ.

4. The Task of the Churches

Common Action by the Churches in Recent Years

Before setting out what we consider to be the task now confronting the Irish Churches we draw attention to the things the Churches and their members have tried to do together in recent years. It would be irrelevant to describe action that has been part of the general ecumenical movement, such as the formation and development of the Irish Council of Churches, the setting up between that Council and the Roman Catholic Hierarchy of the Joint Group under whose auspices this working party has operated, or the inter-church meetings at Ballymascanlon. It must be said, however, that the crisis of violence we are experiencing has affected these developments both by increasing suspicion of the ecumenical movement on the part of those who dislike it and by increasing the sense of urgency felt by those who support it. We confine our treatment to actions directly related to violence or to the political background from which it arises.

Perhaps the first example of formal common action on the part of the Churches, including the Roman Catholic Church, came in the late 1960's when a request was made to the then Prime Minister of Northern Ireland, Captain Terence O'Neill, to receive a deputation to discuss religious provisions in the New University of Ulster. The contacts made at that time enabled the four Churches very early in 1969 to set up what came to be called the *ad hoc* committee whose task was to advise the respective Church leaders on possible joint action with regard to peace. To some extent the way had been prepared for this by the work of the Churches' Industrial Council which, at a less exalted level, had built up unprecedented forms of co-operation in the field of its concern. An approach by the Irish Council of Churches to Cardinal Conway following the Burntollet affair led to the *ad hoc* committee, while another at the same time to Captain O'Neill was not without considerable effect in the decision to set up the Cameron Commission.

Consultation between the leaders of the Churches continued at intervals after these events but it was not until Christmas 1974 that the extent and significance of the common action really made an impact on the general public. Then was launched the Church Leaders' Peace Campaign. The Cardinal, the Primate, the Moderator and President issued a common appeal for peace. They appeared together on television, placed full page advertisements in the press, met the Secretary of State, the Prime Minister and the Taoiseach, and were in conference together seventeen times in the course of a few weeks. Never before had the Churches been seen to co-operate together so openly and so vigorously on a public issue. Rallies in Belfast and other towns revealed many thousands willing and anxious to follow their lead. In the week that this campaign was launched came—fortuitously or providentially —the news of the encounter at Feakle described on pp. 39-40. At first it seemed that this coincidence would confuse the public and perhaps undermine the Church Leaders' Campaign, but eventually it became clear that this practical step had reinforced in the public mind the appeal of the Church Leaders and had exemplified ways in which individual Christians could respond to the appeal put out by the official leaders. The Churches were seen more clearly in a reconciling role than ever before.

The 'cease fire' that followed these events proved a disappointment. It is too early to apportion responsibility for the failure of the community to take full advantage of a lull that might have enabled surer foundations for peace to be laid. That the Churches have a common cause in seeking justice without violence, rather than being identified with sides in the conflict, was more clearly demonstrated by these events than at any previous time.

Common Action by Members of the Churches

On a semi-official level there have been numerous peace marches, meetings and movements which have owed their origin directly or indirectly to Church inspiration and support. It would be impossible to list all the groupings which have been at work and the influence of which has had some bearing on the level of violence. We may mention the Corrymeela Community, the Assisi Fellowship, PACE, Women Together, People Together, the Servite Priory at Benburb; and in the Republic the Glencree Reconciliation Centre, Peace Point and Working for Peace. All of these have had specific Christian and indeed frequently Church-based inspiration.

In addition to all of these, there have been and still are many community-based organisations—

some indeed with connections with paramilitary organisations. Many have engaged people in constructive activity and thinking and this too has had its beneficial effects. Housing Associations have been founded. Holiday schemes have proliferated. Youth work of many kinds has been started. Many of these projects have received help from the Inter-Church Emergency Fund, especially supported by the European Council of Churches, which is operated jointly by representatives of the Irish Council of Churches and the Irish Hierarchy.

In addition to all the work that has been listed, attention must also be given to the work of such movements as the Irish Association, the Social Study Conference and the New Ulster Movement. While in no way church sponsored, these movements have been largely supported by people with a Christian commitment. All of them have done much to stimulate new thought and to produce a more civilised attitude to life. Papers produced for and by them have had some effect on the political and social thinking of the period. The leadership of the Trade Union Movement has also contributed much, especially in the reduction of sectarian strife in places of employment.

Reference must also be made to considerable action by individual Church members and clergy. This kind of thing has been seen over and over again in crisis situations, whether in relief centres, rehabilitation work, attempts to influence industrial workers or approaches to men of violence. Much of this has been done unnoticed and there is reason to believe that much more has been done than the public realises.

Thus there has been a very considerable amount

of action and much more of it has been in common than at previous periods of tension. There are now many more bridges across the divide, although violence has deepened for many the rift itself. Those bridges are there to be crossed and if they can be maintained will some day be busy and significant traffic arteries across which the separated communities may travel to a place of reconciliation.

A programme for the Churches

We consider now what positive involvement and action is required from the Churches in Ireland and from their members, as their specific contribution to the elimination of violence and the achievement of reconciliation.

Violence, while often emanating from a sense of injustice, more easily breeds in an environment of fear, suspicion, bitterness and ignorance. This is the kind of environment that sectarianism inevitably produces, and by sectarianism we mean the frame of mind that exploits denominational differences to promote a sense of superiority, a denial of rights, a justification of conflict.

The Irish Churches have until recently been slow to recognise that total religious segregation is by no means a necessary nor a desirable consequence of legitimate denominational differences; nor is it an acceptable protection for religious beliefs. All organisations and bodies, not excluding the Churches themselves and certainly including those orders with religious or quasi-religious conditions of membership, must ask themselves fearlessly to what extent their actions and stances, no matter what their theological foundation, may contribute to the separation which can produce the terrible

71

results that have occurred in recent years. The Churches have not adequately faced up to the fact and to the consequences of this religious segregation. They have not been vigorous enough or courageous enough in promoting social contacts and dialogue, especially at the level of ordinary people. Lack of contact, lack of dialogue breed an environment of fear, suspicion, ignorance and prejudice, which can rightly be termed sectarian. It is to the elimination of this whole frame of mind that the combined efforts of the Churches need to be directed. Ireland needs a programme to combat sectarianism wherever it is found.

We seek now to make some concrete proposals, basing them on some general principles of Christian action :

(1) The Churches and their members must *act justly themselves.*

In the first instance they must ensure that justice is done and seen to be done within and between the Churches themselves. As St. Augustine said, the Church is called to be 'the reconciled world' and must be seen to be this in the exercise of authority and co-responsibility both within each denomination and between the Churches.

In the wider community the Churches must no less be seen to act justly, not seeking unjustifiable privileges for themselves or giving support by action or by omission to forms of injustice in the community. There is a temptation to remain silent about injustices in order to secure political support for the Church herself in the furtherance of her policies: denunciations of injustice might be omitted for fear of antagonising political leaders or of alienating certain interests or groups within congregations.

Whenever the question is raised whether the actions or policies of the Churches are inherently just, it is needful that the most careful reconsideration be given, not only to ensure that the action is just in the eyes of the Church or Churches themselves, but also to ascertain why it may seem unjust to others, and to remove misunderstandings.

(2) The Churches and their members must *uncover injustice fearlessly* whether perpetrated by political institutions or by others interests or groups in the community. To do so fearlessly and effectively will require :

(a) being careful and accurate in the obtaining and assessment of the facts;

(b) harnessing all possible support within the Churches and the community for active propagation of the facts;

(c) witnessing to justice and acting against injustice and violence.

The suggestion has been put to us that we need an Irish Centre of Christian Social Investigation which, on an all-Ireland basis, perhaps in collaboration with the Universities and other bodies, would provide a means by which the Irish Churches could together probe the nature of 20th Century social situations and find guidelines for concerted Christian action. We commend this idea to the Churches, whether it take the form of a permanent institution or of a series of studies. In addition to the long-term social and economic problems to which attention would be given, we suggest the following as some of the matters which urgently need consideration in the immediate situation of violence whether by such an agency or in some

73

other way :

   (a) The continuous monitoring of progress made in removing the basic grievances of discrimination and injustice within civil society that are related to the occurrence of violence. In particular the effectiveness of new legislation on fair employment should be kept under observation.

   (b) The alerting of the Churches to the danger of permitting their worship to be exploited for political or for military reasons.

It is easy to move from the position that support is due to the State in upholding justice to the position that anything goes if it is authorised by the State. Some of our members urge that it is high time that the ceremonial relationship of the Churches and the Armed Forces (displaying of colours in Churches, blessing of weapons, status and role of chaplains) received radical reconsideration. All would agree that organisations perpetrating violence in Ireland make free use of military symbolism to justify themselves in their own eyes and those of their compatriots; hence there exists a real danger where the Churches appear to extol the military virtues without making the most rigorous distinctions.

A particular aspect of this problem that constantly arises in Ireland is the part played by the Churches when men of violence are accorded funerals in which there is an imitation of the honours paid to members of the security forces killed on duty. Without denying the right of Christian burial, we recommend that clergy of all denominations should take the utmost care to avoid identifying themselves or their Churches with processions and demonstrations of a para-military nature; and, in particular, that the Service used should in no way differ from that used in the case of an ordinary parishioner. We commend the courage of those who have already followed this course.

(c) A critical re-appraisal of the growing counter-insurgency role of the Armed Forces in both North and South.

The danger of defence forces becoming step by step a means of systematic repression is a real one and the Churches could do the community a service by encouraging an impartial scrutiny of such possible developments. It might even be appropriate to form observer teams to monitor army activity vis-a-vis the civilian population in terms of its behaviour and methods. This could be as good a protection for the forces against misrepresentation as for the public against abuse of power.

In making these proposals we do not overlook the good work that has been done and is being done by Christians, active in public affairs. There is a fine tradition of Christian social action in Ireland and abroad, to which often insufficient publicity is given, but a greater measure of corporate action by the Churches in this sphere is called for. It would require courage, patience and perseverance. It may well carry risks and even dangers when it is seen as criticism of certain political institutions or of revolutionary bodies. Both those in power and those opposed to them constantly resist criticism and distort or suppress information.

In certain circumstances it may become necessary for Christian action to take the form of peaceful demonstrations. If so, the greatest care must be taken to avoid violence or the provocation of violence.

If it should prove impracticable to set up a Centre for the study of these issues, the issues themselves must not be neglected by the Churches.

(3) The Churches must be prepared to *come to the aid of victims of injustice.*

Whole areas of public concern have been neglected by the Churches and too often pioneer work has been left to those with little church connection or to people totally opposed to Christianity. Here, as in protest against injustice, it will usually be more effective if the Churches are able to act together, showing compassion from and to both sides. In recent years this kind of work has been undertaken by many reconciliation groups like People Together, Women Together, PACE, Peace Point, Pax Christi, Witness for Peace, Fellowship of Prayer for Christian Unity, and the local branch of the Fellowship of Reconciliation; and by more permanent centres like the Servite Priory at Benburb, the Corrymeela Community and the more recently opened centre at Glencree. While Christian people have played a large part in these efforts, there should be more positive encouragement at an official level by the Churches themselves.

The meeting of material need through direct Church philanthropy has remained largely a denominational matter. A more united approach to it may well entail helping needy people even when the Churches cannot approve all their actions and opinions. For there are people in need of help, caught up in the evils of our society, some of them indoctrinated in evil ways from their tender years. The Churches should not confine their advocacy to groups or causes which it is currently fashionable to espouse, but should seek also to be the voice of those who have no one else to speak for them. Excellent illustrations of such non-violent protest and the best means of promoting it are to be found in 'Non-Violent Action' (a report of the United Reformed Church) and in Jacques Ellul 'Violence'.

Paramount in the Churches' long-term concern for social action in the last quarter of the 20th century must be support for the family and provision for youth. We have seen in bitter experience the demoralisation of the latter following the disintegration of the former. The rehabilitation of family life, with sufficient parental control to prevent the exploitation of younger members by pernicious influences outside, will call for persistent effort in social fields. The strong advocacy and encouragement of Christian standards for mutual love and support within the family are more likely to be effective if steps are taken to secure proper housing for all and the means of earning a reasonable family income, to accord to more equal partnership in the home and outside it to women, to prepare young people for the responsibilities of marriage and parenthood, to achieve greater co-operation between parents on the one hand and schools, churches and youth organisations on the other, and to give more opportunity for the generations to find enjoyment together outside the home.

There is a need, indeed, for women to be included in decisions governing permanent social change. They must be encouraged to take their rightful, confident place in society. They must contribute to the decision-making process not because they are women but because they are equal members of society.

While we emphasise the need for closer bonds within the family as a whole, it would not do to suppose that teenage youngsters will not seek a measure of independence from their parents. It is in this connection that the importance of organisations to which they can belong 'in their own right', as it were, must be seen. It has been very easy to recruit youngsters into bodies with a destructive or partisan object, which may give them a sense of purpose and development. To set up organisations with a constructive aim and to get young people of all backgrounds to join them and participate actively calls for personal qualities of tact and leadership of a high order. Those of our members with direct experience in this field emphasise that the youth organisations are still far from attaining this goal and that new and radical experiment is called for. It is one of the tragedies of violence that the growth of shared youth club activities has been largely brought to a halt. The aim in this whole area must be to bring about reconciliation and growth in mutual understanding and mutual acceptance. In so far as this begins with young people, care must be taken not to produce too abrupt a break with the outlook of parents who may be set in their traditional ways of thinking. Much experimentation and research will be needed to find the most effective means of inspiring whole communities with the new spirit that young people may be brought to adopt. The experience gained in dealing with mixed groups of young people at Corrymeela and elsewhere needs to be applied more generally in permanent situations. There is no doubt that the attainment of a greater accord between the Churches on the subject of mixed marriages would do much to accelerate the growth of shared activities among young people.

Meanwhile in the short term, not least among the victims of injustice, are those who find themselves under duress from the actions of paramilitary forces in their own communities. What is the ordinary man or woman to do when faced with demands for money, pressure to hide contraband material, and perhaps most commonly, the knowledge that to support authority, particularly by the release of information, would bring overwhelming retaliation ? The Churches may well be called upon to face more honestly the problems of conscience involved in these issues. Has it been too readily assumed that the right of self-protection covers acquiescence in anything ? Is Martyrdom the privilege of those who make an idol of their country and is it never to be expected of those who uphold justice or Christian standards of conduct ? What support, moral and material, can the Churches give to those who are prepared to defy not 'the enemy' but the wild men in their own communities? We suggest that violence will in the long run, as a method of action, be overcome by the courage of the non-violent. The Churches, we suggest, have a mission to show this is the greatest of the 'causes' now claiming the support of Irish Christians.

While we recognise that the authorities can make mistakes or be guilty of abuses we recommend that the Churches jointly remind their members that they have a *prima facie* moral obligation to support the currently constituted authorities in Ireland against all para-military forces and that to do so is not in any way to pre-judge longer-term political and constitutional developments. In particular, where an individual has information about illegal activities of para-military organisations, he or she may be assuming a fearsome moral responsibility if, after taking account of all the personal, family and other dangers involved, he does not put such information before the authorities. Furthermore the Churches should be prepared to offer strictly confidential advice through their clergy to their members when faced with these terrible questions.

(4) The Churches should *encourage and prepare their members to take all legitimate action to overcome injustice.*

If their members are to do this effectively they need much more education in the social and political implications of the Gospel than many of them now have. Mindful of our terms of reference, which bid us 'indicate to the Churches how they may best educate their members' in these matters to 'promote the achievement of a society acceptable to the great majority of the people by means which rule out recourse to such violence', we make the following suggestions for a systematic campaign :

(a) That the Religious Education programmes of the Churches should include an adequate treatment of the political and social implications of Christianity for Irish society as well as of the democratic methods available for promoting justice and peace.

(b) That reasoned and readable short articles

on these matters should be prepared for inclusion in parish and congregational magazines.

(c) That Bible study outlines and supporting material relating to these matters be prepared for use in youth and discussion groups.

(d) That conferences be organised at local and regional level at which members of different Churches together study questions of this kind.

(e) That more provision be made in the curricula of theological colleges and seminaries for studies in the Christian attitude to violence, particularly in Irish society, and in non-violent methods of promoting social justice.

(f) That with a view to encouraging continuous thought and action in the field of community relations, efforts be made to raise a capital sum sufficient to provide for :

(i) annual Irish Christian Peace Prizes, to be awarded to groups on each side of the traditional divide a n d to individuals adjudged to have made the most notable contributions to reconciliation in the previous twelve months;

(ii) an annual published popular Lecture on some aspect of the Irish peace problem considered from a Christian point of view;

(iii) scholarships for recognised peace courses at Universities and other approved institutions.

(g) That provision be made for regular reviews of this campaign at, say, three-yearly intervals.

In addition to promoting such a campaign of education for their own members, the Churches should not hesitate to give a direct lead to public opinion on issues of justice. This may mean, for example, the Churches' support for a Bill of Rights to protect various minorities. The Churches can together stand for all political proposals that clearly attack injustice within the community and they can do this while fully recognising that their members have the right to support any legitimate political party. It is, however, quite another thing to support organisations with a political aim that act outside or on the fringe of the law. We cannot indicate too clearly our total opposition to all such action, leading as it inevitably does to violence against the lives and property of the people. There is an evil significance in such campaigns which not only has serious implications for the survival of democratic institutions in all parts of Ireland and further afield, but also results in the immediate perpetration of injustice against large numbers of citizens.

(5) While convinced that Christians should normally seek to promote reform through the normal political processes, we recognise that situations do arise in which such action may be ineffective. The Churches cannot, therefore, escape the obligation *to give guidance to their members about methods of direct action alternative to violence*, and not open to the same condemnation. The general ineffectiveness of violence in Northern Ireland that we have noted in Chapters 2 and 3, suggests that this would not only have the advan-

tage of avoiding loss of life but also that of achieving results.

In the past, the Churches have often played a leading role in supporting and pioneering new methods of social advance and social welfare. They now need to play a similar role in the development of new methods of corporate self-expression on the part of those who suffer from injustice amounting to oppression. One of the weaknesses of the Christian appeal to non-violence has been the gap between exhortation and the availability of a sufficient range of non-violent means, methods and expertise accessible to those who need it. The following suggestions have been made to the Working Party by some of its members :

(a) The sponsoring of small groups of experienced and adequately trained Christians, preferably on an Inter-Church basis, a task force available to anyone interested in bringing about just changes through non-violent means.

(b) An assessment of the effectiveness of the Churches' involvement in conflict situations in the past five years in Northern Ireland, not with a view to apportioning blame or otherwise, but essentially to learn from past achievements and mistakes with a view to encouraging non-violent methods in the search for a just society.

(c) A Church-supported programme of training and education in peace work and in non-violent philosophy and methods. This would involve the preparation and use of suitable material at all levels in the educational system, from the theological colleges and seminaries of the Churches themselves (where we should in any case look for much closer co-operation and common study than in the past), to the programmes of religious education in the secondary, primary and Sunday schools.

(d) The need for the police to receive training in non-violent techniques and more instruction than they at present receive on community needs and civil rights, is something to which the Churches might draw attention.

The above suggestions relate to direct action of a non-violent kind. But direct action that is violent exists among us in fact. There are within the para-military organisations on both sides of the conflict men and women who claim to be Christians and who do not accept, in the present conditions in Ireland, a restriction of the use of force in all circumstances to what is sanctioned by the State. If such people decide to act in accordance with their conviction, ought not the Churches to point out to them that they continue to be bound by moral norms ? The Working Party itself unequivocally condemns the continuance of violent campaigns but nevertheless asks whether those involved in them should not attempt to investigate and promulgate norms of conduct for themselves.

This would be in some ways analogous to conventions already governing formal military action and might include such matters as respect for non-combatants, the right to resign from para-military organisations, the outlawing of intimidation and torture, the status of prisoners. Many would argue that such a convention would only slightly ameliorate conditions at the expense of recognising terrorists. Others contend that to mitigate the effects of a disease you cannot yet cure is good medicine. (6) The most distinctive task confronting the Churches is to *promote and support reconciliation.* 'God . . . has committed unto us the ministry of reconciliation'. The Churches must engage in the task of evangelism in a renewed effort to open men's hearts to the grace and truth of Christ. From this source can come forgiveness, patience, peace and reconciliation. Violence is an assault upon a brother made in the image of God and redeemed by Christ. 'We recognise that this is primarily the reconciliation of men to God, but men cannot be reconciled to God unless they are reconciled to one another (1 John 4: 20-21). The Churches must constantly remind their own members and others of the need for reconciliation. We recognise also that the reconciliation of men to one another means little unless it be accompanied by a common determination to remedy injustice . . . It is not enough for individuals to show goodwill unless an unjust system is changed'. (Non-Violent Action, page 5).

Reconciliation will mean acknowledging our own sins, being ready to forgive wrongs done against us and recognising that we have all, as individuals and institutions, things to repent of — acts of omission, words ill-spoken and acquiescence in evil acts. We have not been the salt of the earth and the light of the world and have not expressed our faith in terms of social relationships.

We turn now to live issues that have caused misunderstanding between the Churches and concerning which a closer accord would contribute to the cause of reconciliation.

Mixed Marriages are a matter of considerable

pastoral concern. Participants in such marriages, especially where they occur in situations of acute community tension, are particularly liable to be victimised. These circumstances, especially prevalent in Northern Ireland, should not be ignored in the examination of the procedures and rules for mixed marriages in the local context. We draw these circumstances to the attention of the Joint Committee set up to monitor practice in this matter.

Separated Education : The question of an 'integrated' system of education is being increasingly canvassed and cannot be passed over in silence. Members of our Working Party are not in agreement upon this issue. We confine ourselves in this Report to conclusions in the matter of education on which we are agreed. We are in agreement that the Churches should promote pilot schemes and research projects to find effective ways of bringing together Protestant and Catholic young people at school level. Such schemes could include exchanges of teachers between Catholic and Protestant schools (particularly in sensitive areas of the curriculum, such as history, civics, Irish language and culture, history of the Churches in Ireland and in the promotion of joint projects and field work in relevant subjects). Shared Sixth Form Colleges have been suggested. Common nursery schools in suitable areas could be developed. This would give mothers opportunities of meeting which it would otherwise be difficult to bring about. Debates, cultural and folk-cultural exhibitions and other extra-curricular activities can often usefully be shared. Games and athletics are also areas for sharing and this can be further developed. The different traditions in regard to games which have tended to characterise the two communities will need diversification so as to increase sharing.

The teaching of Religion in schools of both traditions must have explicitly and deliberately an ecumenical dimension. The stereotypes which each community may have inherited regarding the religious beliefs and practices of the other must be firmly rejected and replaced by exact and sympathetic understanding. It will often be desirable to invite representatives of the other traditions to come to the school to talk about their own tradition.

In discussion and planning for sharing at school level care should be taken to respect sincerely held convictions on one side or the other. It would be a pity if something which is intended to promote reconciliation were allowed to become instead a new subject of controversy and dissension.

We recommend the establishment of a Joint Committee, consisting m a i n l y of practising teachers, but with representatives of diocesan and area education authorities and of parents, to consider in detail the implementation of the above suggestions.

(7) *Community Development and Reconciliation*

There will be much scope for an educative role as groups feel their way towards the fulfilment of their aims in a more integrated society. Here the Churches may well exercise their influence not only on the formal provision that is made for adult education, which may well assume a growing importance in the light of these developments, but also in its own educational work and in that undertaken by the community action groups themselves. In that way the Churches can help in the process of releasing the latent forces in the community of goodwill, enterprise, concern and talent which may have been unexploited or unrecognised.

For too long society maintained some sort of order by restraining the energies of the under-privileged or canalising them solely into physical w o r k. Reconciliation means accepting those energies, developing them and seeking to integrate them constructively into the building of a just social order with which all can identify.

Meanwhile there is an immediate practical situation in which an immediate ministry of recon-ciliation has to be exercised. We suggest that the direct application of the ideal of reconciliation to our present predicament includes :

(i) That all political leaders should be encouraged to see their task as that of reaching a just agreement with their opponents rather than of achieving victory over them; and that to this end they should be open to any reasonable settlement proposed.

(ii) That all people of good will should use their votes and their influence to encourage the politicians to see things that way.

(iii) That all people of good will, and political leaders in particular, should use their influence to ensure that paramilitary action on both sides is progressively eliminated from the scene.

(iv) That all should support the just use of the State's authority in both parts of Ireland to restrain those who refuse to abandon violent practices.

(v) That in every possible way, including those suggested in this report, and remembering that joint action is in itself a source of enhanced mutual knowledge and understanding, the Churches and their members should *act together* in support of the call made together by their leaders
to talk, to think, to pray peace.

We conclude by reiterating the futility of calling for reconciliation and peace in the community in the absence of full reconciliation between the Churches themselves. In facing the consequences of speaking and acting against the men of violence, the Churches may indeed have to endure a phase of persecution as the price of any real influence for the Faith in years to come. Whether that be so or not, if the Churches are true to their Lord they will individually and *jointly* lift up their hearts in prayer for guidance and help, and do together all that conscience does not compel them to do separately. Both in their corporate acts and in the conduct of their members, the Churches must now demonstrate that a reconciled relationship between them has become a constant factor in Irish society.

Summary of Conclusions and Recommendations

1. In spite of the complicated historical and social issues involved and without prejudice to any legitimate political aim, we find unanimously that there is no justification in the present situation in Ireland for the existence of any para-military organisations. (Chapter 1, page 17).

2. It follows that we see no justification for the campaigns of bombing and killing being carried on in Northern Ireland, in the Republic of Ireland and in Britain. (Chapter 1, pages 17-18).

3. We uphold the right of any group to express its views in peaceful demonstration and in seeking electoral support (Chapter 3, page 65).

4. We recommend that the Churches actively support peace and reconciliation movements. (Chapter 4, page 76).

5. While we recognise that the authorities can make mistakes or be guilty of abuses, we recommend that the Churches jointly remind their members that they have a *prima facie* moral obligation to support the currently constituted authorities in Ireland against all para-

military powers and that to do so is not in any way to prejudge longer-term political and constitutional developments. In particular, where an individual has information about violent activities of paramilitary organisations he or she may be assuming a personal moral responsibility if, after taking account of all the personal, family and other dangers involved, he does not put such information before the authorities. Furthermore the Churches should be prepared to offer strictly confidential advice through their clergy to their members when faced with these terrible questions. (Chapter 4, pages 79-80).

6. We recommend that the Churches support the principle of a Bill of Rights to protect minorities. We are in favour of extending the functions of the Commissioner of Complaints in Northern Ireland. (Chapter 4, page 82).

7. We suggest the setting up of a Christian Centre of Social Investigation which would conduct research into problems underlying social and communal unrest and would monitor continuously progress made in removing the basic grievances of discrimination and injustice within civil society that are related to the occurrence of violence. Other problems to be investigated underlie our further recommendations and they are problems which must not be shelved if such a centre cannot be established. (Chapter 4, page 73).

8. We recommend action by the Churches to ensure that their worship is not exploited by paramilitary organisations at funerals and commemorations. (Chapter 4, pages 74-75).

9. We recommend all possible support for the family as a social unit, both through Christian pastoral care and through practical measures set out in the Report. (Chapter 4, pages 77-78).

10. We recommend urgent experiment and enterprise in the Youth Service designed to make an appeal to those sections of youth hitherto not attracted to its activities. We urge further effort to establish and maintain interdenominational activities for youth. (Chapter 4, pages 78-79).

11. We hold that the Churches should set an example to society in the place they give to women thus encouraging them to take their rightful, confident place in society. (Chapter 4, page 78).

12. We call for a sustained and far reaching programme of education within the Churches themselves by which their members may be made more aware of the political and social implications of Christianity for Irish society as well as of the democratic methods available for promoting justice and peace. (Chapter 4, pages 80-82).

13. We urge upon the attention of the Joint Committee appointed to monitor mixed marriages the special circumstances existing in Northern Ireland. (Chapter 4, pages 85-86).

14. We recommend the establishment of a Joint Committee to consider closer contact and co-operation between Roman Catholic and other schools. (Chapter 4, page 87).

15. We regard the growth of community awareness in many areas as potentially one of the more positive developments of recent years and we urge local congregations to make every effort to play a part in these developments. (Chapter 4, page 83 and pages 87-88).

16. We suggest that all political leaders should be encouraged to see their task as that of reaching a just agreement with their opponents rather than of achieving victory over them; and that to this end they should be open to any reasonable settlement proposed. (Chapter 4, pages 88-89).

Appendix

The working party has commissioned short research statements from representatives of each of the main denominations and these are printed below.

The Church of Ireland attitude to violence

The recent and growing concern about the role of the Church of Ireland in the political, economic and social life of the island, has to be seen against the background and extent of the changing Church involvement in society and of the changes in that society. This can best be illustrated by the decision of the Standing Committee of the General Synod in 1970 to appoint a Committee 'to study the positive role of the Church in all aspects of political, social and economic life in Ireland and to report back from time to time'. The appointment of this Committee was occasioned by the disturbances in Northern Ireland in the years 1968 and 1969.

The following extracts have been taken from those sections of the reports made annually to the Synod by the Role of the Church Committee (as the body set up in 1970 has come to be called), in which reference is made to the problems of violence.

1970 : We warmly welcome the programme of social reforms introduced in Northern Ireland.

We believe that this programme should meet reasonable needs and grievances and that it is a basis for a more just and peaceful society.

But we know that legislation by itself cannot change society. This needs the interest, concern and goodwill of all sections of the community. We therefore urge members of the Church of Ireland to give their wholehearted support to these reforms. Further we believe that the reforms deserve and should have the support of all right-thinking people. This is the only way forward in Northern Ireland and it means the renunciation of prejudice, bigotry and intolerance by all sections of the community.

We reiterate our abhorrence of violence and all forms of intimidation.

1971 : We believe that in Ireland there is no excuse for violence or intimidation, and we condemn both outright. At the moment of preparing this Report we are particularly grieved and shocked by the callous killing of five men on Brougher Mountain. Such episodes have darkened our history.

We also express our disquiet at the alleged use of public funds to purchase firearms for the destruction of fellow Irishmen, and the excessive availability of arms for illegal purposes throughout Ireland, North and South.

1972 : The Committee expresses sincere sympathy with all who have suffered in any way as a result of violence.

We are perturbed by statements occasionally made by some professing Christians who hold positions of influence in the community, in which it would appear that an attempt is made to place the active pursuit of violence, under certain circumstances, in a more favourable light than is compatible with Christian moral standards.

Nothing in Northern Ireland or the Republic of Ireland justifies a deliberately calculated and planned policy of violence designed to achieve political or social ends by a reign of terror. This has no mandate from our Lord.

The results of planned violence, especially in Ireland today, are to be seen not only in the death or suffering caused to unfortunate victims but in the triumph of malice and hatred and the moral degradation of those who perpetrate it.

The Committee is gravely concerned about the prevalence of intimidation, including the effect on the administration of the law, and urges the whole community, North and South, to support the R.U.C. and Gardai in the discharge of their duties in a very difficult situation. There must also be gratitude not only to police but to all public servants, soldiers, firemen and ambulance workers, whose duties involve them in great danger, and an appreciation of the suffering of their wives and families.

The members were agreed in regretting the use of internment but recognised the difficulty involved in releasing people amongst whom there are those who might organise violence and inflict suffering. We look forward to the time when conditions in the community will lead to the end of internment.

The Committee welcomes the investigation of all allegations of torture and brutality.

Yet a warning must be given. There is a double standard in much recent thinking, speaking, and writing which justifies actions on the part of one section of the community while condemning similar actions on the part of another. There must be total condemnation of ALL killing and wounding, the infliction of mental and moral anguish, and particularly the suffering and involvement of children. Revenge contradicts the Christian Gospel.

The majority of Northern people, so often in their persons and property the main target for attack, have spurned retaliation. We wholeheartedly commend their persistent restraint.

1973 : The Report referred to the Statement made by the Archbishops of Armagh and Dublin, on the occasion of the publication of the British Government's White Paper on Northern Ireland, and quoted from the Statement.

We therefore urge all people to adopt a constructive approach and to avoid words and actions that would wreck the present attempt to take us out of our violence and instability.

There is no justification for violence in any of its forms from any source in our present situation. We, therefore, welcome especially the firm resolve of the White Paper to establish the rule of law as a compelling priority.

The Committee welcomes and supports whole-heartedly the January, 1973, condemnation by the four Church leaders of sectarian and political marches, whether of civilians or security personnel. The appeal which they made to bring this evil practice to an end deserves and should receive full support from all responsible citizens.

One of the most significant developments of the troubled situation in Northern Ireland since 1969 has been the re-emergence of organised bodies of private individuals who have embarked on activities of a para-military nature while claiming s o m e allegiance to political ideals. It is difficult to over-estimate t h e importance o f the existence of these private armies which exercise considerable influence within the community and which have been able to impose their will and purpose upon much of the Province.

Such bodies have received much publicity and differing reasons have been advanced for their existence. Condemnation of such groups is generally linked with comments upon the dangers of extremism and it is suggested that all discussion of these phenomena should be viewed in the general context of social and political conditions which permit such private armies to exist. But it should be remembered that in many areas of the Province membership of a paramilitary organisation represents for some the natural expression of political frustration at a time when the normal democratic process appears to them to have ceased to operate.

We would accordingly emphasise the danger inherent in prohibiting any political groups from putting forward candidates for elections. Such prohibition may well play into the hands of the men of violence.

The activities of private armies are in fact only one manifestation of conditions where 'violence-politics' appear to be successful. The niceties of moral judgment do not enter into the thinking of many ordinary people living in conditions where law and order have broken down and where traditional political institutions no longer seem to have any relevancy. To discuss the Christian ethic of violence may be a comparatively easy task in general terms, but in the current tensions of Northern Ireland thousands of people are involved in situations where fear and apprehension have clouded judgments and it seems clear that great care ought to be exercised in the framing of any pro- nouncements which do not take account of this important fact.

None of these factors provides justification

for individuals to take it upon themselves to operate outside the law in the present situation, nor compel fellow citizens to adopt a particular attitude because of fear or intimidation, nor deprive them of their homes and jobs, nor to challenge the authority of the forces of law and order. Any action which is taken by individuals and which by its nature removes them from the ambit of the law, compels the Church to consider whether such action is not just illegal but immoral.

1974 : Since the last report of this committee, the question of violence and death has continued to be the tragic pre-occupation of Irishmen. Many have died and many more have been injured. The damage to property has continued to mount.

The attention of the Committee has been drawn particularly to the sufferings of families living in the immediate area of the border, both north and south.

It is within the context of violence and the continuing pre-occupation with this tragedy that the committee considered the Sunningdale Communiqué. The Committee recognises that within our Church diverse political outlooks are to be found. It is important to note this fact. But the committee would stress that with the continuing tragic toll of death and destruction the Sunningdale Communiqué could represent a major step towards a peaceful solution if, and only if, it can be seen to be implemented by all the parties in an atmosphere of trust and courage. Particular urgency is attached to the active pursuit by security forces, unfettered by political considerations alone, of wrong doers; the ending of support, sanctuary or sympathy for men of violence from whatever source they come or to which they flee. The acts of terrorism may be perpetrated by a small minority, but there are many more who accept violence as a method of enforcing political change. Others are complacent. In general there is too much reluctance to accept the restrictions a n d inconvenience involved in countering and controlling the terrorist campaigns. The demand for a greater commitment to ending crimes of violence and the sacrifices needed to achieve that end can be made without reservation or hesitation because of the implementation of the social reforms in Northern Ireland.

Blanket condemnations and sympathy are not enough. Included in the appendices was a collection of comments and statements on the present situation by Bishops of the Church of Ireland.

1975 : The Committee warmly welcomed the action of the Primate and the other Church leaders who launched the Joint Peace Campaign in December. This unique campaign was motivated by a shared concern over the violence and its consequences, and was aimed at 'every home in the land', and at 'all who advocate or indulge in violence'. The Church leaders, expressing appreciation of the efforts of many groups and individuals towards peace, called on people to 'Think, Pray, Talk Peace'. The response was immediate and overwhelming from all corners of Ireland. Responses took various forms, some being organised by groups and some by individuals. The cease-fire was greeted with much relief and thankfulness. The Church leaders visited heads of Government in Stormont, Westminster and Dublin to keep them informed and to encourage policies that would take advantage of the prevailing favourable climate of opinion.

Representatives of the Committee had interviews with the Minister for Justice in the Republic, later with the Opposition spokesman on Justice and some of his Front Bench colleagues to express their deep concern about the urgent need to implement fully and quickly the agreement at Sunningdale 'That persons committing crimes of violence, however motivated, in any part of Ireland should be brought to trial irrespective of the part of Ireland in which they are located.

The attitude of the Church of Ireland may be aptly summed up in the words of the Primate, the Most Rev. G. O. Simms, Archbishop of Armagh, in November, 1973 : 'I again condemn unreservedly all acts of terrorism whether perpetrated by or on Roman Catholics or Protestants in the name of one organisation or another, be it an illegal organisation or not. I want only to see peace in our land.'

The Methodist attitude to violence

The Methodist people, since the days of John Wesley, have prided themselves on being 'the friends of all and the enemies of none'. This claim goes back to the days of persecution and the experiences derived from being a small minority community.

In Ireland, however, the Methodists instinctively and naturally regarded themselves as being very much part of the Protestant population. They undoubtedly over the years sought to live at peace and in understanding with their Roman Catholic contemporaries. There are many references in official documents to that desire. But in times of communal or national stress there was never any doubt as to where the Church's sympathies lay.

Perhaps the fairest summary of Methodist attitudes during the years 1869-1960 would be : 1). Good will and a concern for good relationships when the country is free from tension. 2). Concern, and disapproval of violence, when the Home Rule movement is most active. 3). An implicit suggestion that basic liberties go hand in hand with the maintenance of link with the Crown. 4). The concerns to which reference is most frequently made have to do with drink, gambling and Sunday observance. 5). A seeming unawareness—or at best a very occasional recognition — of the social ills that contribute to and exacerbate community unrest e.g. bad housing, unemployment, low wages and other unsatisfactory social conditions. 6). In Northern Ireland general approval and support, though not uncritical. 8). A recurring, though not frequently asserted, fear and suspicion of Roman Catholic stances and claims.

From 1960 onwards the statements of the Conference on public affairs may be listed as follows :

1962   Questioning capital punishment.

1963   Unemployment in Northern Ireland.

1964   Grateful for better community relations.

1965   Support for O'Neill-Lemass meeting.

1966   Four page document to (a) safeguard faith, (b) maintain and live out Christian doctrine of reconciliation, (c) promote just society including an end to discrimination, (d) civil powers to uphold justice and righteousness, (e) requirement to obey civil power in all proper regulations.

1967   Pamphlet on relations with W.C.C., Roman Catholic Church and Roman Catholics. Fullest possible co-operation without compromise urged.

1970   Three page document on present situation in Ireland.

(A)   1. Re-affirmation of previous declaration : (a) Obligation to demonstrate to all irrespective of faith, qualities of love found in Christ. Need to make bitterness disappear from Irish life. (b) Any form of discrimination based on creed, etc., contrary to God's will. Call to remove all injustice. (c) Call to civil powers to exert authority without fear or favour in pursuit of justice. (d) All are required to obey duly constituted authorities call for support of civil powers in proper regulations designed to promote better relationships.

2. Welcome further reforms in Northern Ireland. Urges speedy implementation. Reforms considered adequate to remove most of the grievances felt by the minority. Call for political leaders to emulate Church leaders in joint call to peace, mutual understanding and common effort.

3. Summer season traditionally period for parades, etc. Mature society should be able to allow all sections to demonstrate points of view within the law. Call however to those organising parades and demonstrations to weigh carefully what is involved before they exercise their rights — particularly in or near tension areas. Party tunes near places of worship. Organisers cannot wash hands of responsibility if violence results.

4. Obligation of politicians in Northern Ireland and Republic to speak and act with full sense of responsibility. Appeals to religious prejudice are betrayal of common humanity. Votes gained at cost of strife are bought with human suffering.

5. Call to vote with full awareness of responsibility and to consider character of candidates in light of preceding paragraphs.

6. Deep concern at reports of illegal import of arms. Welcome to declaration by Republic denouncing use of physical force.

(B)   Condemnation of spirit and act of murder.

(1) Members of secret organisations urged to consider duty to God before that owed to Ireland or Britain.

(2) Those who traditionally glorify use of unlawful force should think again.

(3) Take gun out of Irish politics. Gunmen cannot survive if public support and sympathy are withdrawn.

(C)   Community relations.

Abandon recriminations about the past. Take positive action. No betrayal of conviction to work together in matters of agreed common concern.

(1) Promote dialogue between neighbouring church groups.

(2) Support local community and peace groups.

(3) Call to participate in political life—but little hope for future peace while political parties seen specifically linked to religious divisions.

(4) Support joint bodies, e.g. Samaritans, Churches' Industrial Council.

(5) Deal specifically with housing problem.

(6) Particular emphasis on training and welfare, provision for unemployed youth.

(7) Extend youth service so as to increase contacts across divisions in our society.

(D)   Misuse of drugs.

1971   Call to all men, irrespective of creed or political conviction to work together for common good. Call for joint Protestant - R.C. Committee, also to include top level Government representation. This Committee should issue public statements. Need to bring children up free from prejudice. Rights of all within the law to propagate religious and political ideals. Justice of a fair sharing by all in the responsibility of government. Value of regular loving prayer for reconciliation. Assurance of support to Methodists who are members of Trade Unions, Orange and Black Institutions, if they try to persuade their organisations to act in the best interests of the whole community. Reformation faith best maintained by personal witness. Support for regulations necessary to maintain peace. Support for recent statements by Church leaders condemning violence.

1972   Sex education in day schools.

1973   Call to use votes in Assembly elections responsibly. Try to secure stable democratic society. Ballot box must replace violence and civil disturbance. Violence can only harden attitudes. Welcome to growing demand for cease-fire.

Long report on drug abuse.

1974   Danger of supporting movements and organisations which are not subject to normal checks of public criticism and which act in defiance of law and use intimidation. Commend politicians who seek solution to present troubles in positive and constitutional ways.

Need for Government and politicians to communicate adequately with common people and to be sensitive to their anxieties and fears.

Urgent need in Northern Ireland for early and satisfactory solution to problem of policing. Call to all to take a stand against intimidation and support police force. Re-affirmation of equality of all men before the law. Right of every man to civil and religious liberty. Right of all elected groups to participate in processes and responsibilities of government or opposition. Belief in the reconciling power of God in Jesus Christ to enable all to live together for the good of all.

1975 Thanks to President and Secretary for part in Church Leaders' Peace Initiative and to Methodist participants in Feakle talks. Emigration. South Africa. Alcohol.

The attitude of the Methodist Church to public issues is officially to be found in decisions taken by the annual Conference on the recommendations of its various committees and in addresses by the Conference to the Methodist people in Ireland and to its sister Conference in Britain. Public statements by the President or by senior officials of the Church are of significance, but cannot be regarded as official in the same way as action and decisions of the Conference. It is, however, always possible that Conference action does not represent necessarily the mind and attitudes of ordinary Church members, so that both official and unofficial statements may be less significant than would at first appear.

Nevertheless it may be argued that, failing evidence to the contrary, the official stances listed above are an indication of the mind of the Church.

The Presbyterian attitude to violence

The attitude of the Presbyterian Church of Ireland to violence, has in the 20th century been shaped by an emphasis on the teaching of Romans 13: 1-7 and 1 Peter 2: 13-17, that the government of a country is divinely ordained and has the right to claim the citizens' respect, support and obedience. It has thus supported the use of force by the state and been opposed to all violence against the state.

Such a theological understanding of the relationship between the state and the citizen, has normally in practice in this period dictated attitudes and actions, to which the majority of Presbyterians would in any case have been committed on purely pragmatic grounds of political aspirations. If political opposition to Home Rule, however, had resulted, as it almost did, in large numbers of Presbyterian people being actively involved in armed rebellion against the government of the day, it is reasonable to assume that Calvinist teaching on the right in the last resort to oppose by force an unjust ruler, would have been explicitly expanded.

It should be noted, however, that having accepted rather than welcomed the settlement of partition, the same attitude to the state was advocated in the Republic of Ireland as in Northern Ireland. Thus even in 1923 the General Assembly passed a resolution in which 'the Assembly notes with pleasure the encouraging progress which has been made towards the restoration of peace in the

Free State and prays for a speedy and complete cessation of any activities aimed at continuing the cruel internecine warfare that has been waged during the last year. The Assembly is fully assured that all the members of the Church within the Free State fulfil the duty of co-operating with the Government as by law established'.

No radical change in attitudes can be seen in the period since the outbreak of the present 'troubles'. In an observation on the Government White Paper, 'Northern Ireland; Constitutional Proposals.', the General Board of the Church stated that :

> Lawless violence must be repudiated. Christians may differ on whether armed force is ever justified; but if it is it should be in defence of life and liberty under the rule of law. It should not be used for the preservation or gaining of privilege, but against men of violence who would impose their will upon an unconsenting community and who are the enemies of all. We consider that nothing in the White Paper violates Christian conscience or justifies any section holding the community to ransom or resorting to violence. (March 1973).

Again and again in the recent years, the Presbyterian Church has on this basis expressed unequivocal opposition to violence and called for support for the security forces. A typical statement was that adopted by the same General Board of the Church in February 1974 :

> We once again unreservedly denounce the acts of violence which continue to disgrace our land, our Christian faith and every honest cause.

Whether such violence arises from political ambition or revenge, whether it is directed against random individuals, specific groups or security personnel, whether it is against private or public property, all must be condemned, and those who engage in it repudiated wholeheartedly no matter from what quarter they come.

The first obligation of the Government should be to give security to those who wish to live in peace and go about their lawful business. However humanly imperfect the forces of law or order may be, they should be given practical assistance by citizens on all sides in their difficult task.

Two things should be noted about this statement :

(a) The consistency of opposition to the use of violence and the taking of law into one's own hands, whether this be by 'republican' or 'loyalist', 'catholic' or 'protestant' groups.

(b) The deep sense of indebtedness to the security forces, a feeling made quite explicit at other times, that they have acted with restraint and courage in the face of severe provocation and bitter vilification; but a sensitivity also, to the fact that the forces of law and order must themselves be subject to law and order. In 1971 the Government Committee of the Church expressed their 'deep concern that the Governments of the United Kingdom and of Northern Ireland should protect persons under detention or internment f r o m unnecessary constraints or violence', at the same time calling on 'Christians not so immediately involved as we are', to 'concern themselves as much for those who live under the shadow of terrorism and subversion as under the shadow of interrogation and detention'. In June 1972 the General Assembly resolved 'to continue to condemn the use of brutality from any quarter; and welcome the instruction of the Secretary of State for Northern Ireland that "there can be no question of brutality in interrogation".'

Recognising the danger of violence begetting violence, the Presbyterian Church has repeatedly charged its people 'in Christ's name . . . not to be goaded by anyone into acts of violence; to struggle unceasingly against any hardening of heart or closing of mind; to stand resolute in their faith and Church throughout any storm; to pray fervently for peace and all things that make for peace in this land; and to act vigorously and perseveringly in accordance with their prayers'. This action was specified at times as a call to take an uncompromising stand against the evil of intimidation, to 'defend their neighbours, even at cost to themselves'; at others as a 'showing restraint and charity towards those of different religious and political persuasions'; yet again as 'persevering discussion between our contending communities, by painstaking recognition of the different interests and ideals among us and by honest readiness for change', etc. All this is explicitly related to the call of the Church 'to engage in the ministry of reconciliation' particularly 'in changing revolutionary situation'.

One of the most encouraging aspects of the Presbyterian stance in this recent period has been an awareness of the Church's partial responsibility for the terrible situation. A statement by the Government Committee in 1969 pointed out that 'in what has happened we are reaping the harvest of mutual suspicion and fear, of non-co-operation, vested interests and party advantage . . . Although our General Assembly and Church have repeatedly spoken out on issues of social injustice and have tried to act in fairness to our fellow citizens of whatever communion, we must confess that we have not done so with sufficient zeal and urgency, sufficient self-examination and self-denial. We have not always loved our neighbour as ourselves and have not infrequently made the conduct of others an excuse for inaction or reaction on our part'.

With this acceptance of responsibility there is expressed also a plea that others, especially 'representatives of the Roman Catholic community' might make a similar declaration 'showing the same concern for the grievances and fears, the lack of confidence and consideration felt by so many of our own people'. This concern for mutuality is a continuing concern expressing itself in this comment of the General Board on the White Paper proposals for Irish co-operation :

As a Church in Ireland, North and South, we should welcome proposals for sincere co-operation between these areas. This, however, must be based on mutual respect and self-determination, not unilateral claims and interventions. Further we fear that the greater the disparity in standing between those taking part in any Council of Ireland drawn from a sovereign parliament and a regional assembly, the less real, confident partnership it offers' (March 1973).

The same concern is expressed in a resolution of the General Assembly in June 1974 where it is stated that 'more regard must be paid outside the Province to the hopes and fears of the majority as well as the minority here. If special political requirements are made, these must have adequate support among those directly affected by them and not just be imposed nationally by majorities not governed by the same requirements'. The strongest expression of this concern was in a statement issued by the Government Committee after the introduction of 'direct rule' in 1972. This stated that :

> We deplore the decision of the United Kingdom Government to prorogue the Northern Ireland Parliament and the consequent denial to democratically elected representatives of the people to a voice in the Government of their country; and we further deplore that this action taken now is above all else at the expense of a peaceful majority who have sought to maintain their cause in an orderly and lawful way.
>
> We speak for a people in Northern Ireland who, without consent, are now suffering a massive deprivation of their constitutional and civil rights and a substantial disfranchisement, exceeding any previous curtailment of local voting rights such as have caused widespread protests in the past. This is being done after they have suffered, patiently and resolutely, prolonged and violent attacks upon them both by hand and tongue. The pain and loss of confidence thus engendered towards those responsible for all this, both in Ireland and beyond, should not be underestimated nor disregarded.

With this passionate concern, there goes however a recognition of the need for change. The 1974 General Assembly was to affirm that 'to provide a framework for order, stability and peaceful development in Northern Ireland it is essential that there should be a sharing of responsibility and power between different sections of the community, who are prepared to act for the community's good'.

In the period of the current 'troubles' the Presbyterian Church has shown an awareness of the need to study in depth the causes of violence in our society. Two important reports presented to the Assembly in 1971 and 1974 were on the themes of 'Radical Change, Reform and Revolution' and 'Republicanism—the aims, ideals and methods of Irish Republicanism'. It has also shown some awareness of the need for social and political change and encouraged its membership to a much more determined effort to understand the viewpoint of the Roman Catholic community and to work with all men of goodwill towards a genuine peace with justice for all. In this it has held to the position outlined at the start of this paper, of calling for support for the security forces of the state and opposing all who would seek change by violent means. There is also a deep concern that 'the effects of five years confrontation and terrorism, of bombings, shootings, burnings, intimidating threats and insults, self-styled armies and paramilitary associations, mass strikes and physical obstruction, must be seen not only for what they have already done, both to individuals and the whole community, but also for the still greater evils to which they lead directly on, politically, economically, socially and religiously' (General Assembly 1974). Because such a situation is intolerable to the Christian conscience, the Church has sought to 'think, pray and work for peace' and in the pursuit of peace to transcend the historic religious divisions of the community. Here the participation of the Presbyterian Church in joint statements by the Church leaders, the Peace campaign, etc., is relevant.

The position outlined here has been that adopted and advocated by the appointed leaders and committees of the Presbyterian Church; and it should be borne in mind that the membership of the Church as a whole might reflect a more conservative political outlook. This factor is represented in the obvious tensions that express themselves in some of the statements, revealing the intense struggle within the Church to find a common Christian viewpoint on matters about which the Church membership may themselves be deeply divided. Though it is difficult to assess, there can be little doubt that the position taken by the Church leaders has had its effect in shaping the views of Presbyterian people in the period under consideration.

The Roman Catholic attitude to violence

In the course of the struggle of the Irish people for political and economic independence, the Irish Catholic Bishops have consistently followed two basic principles in guiding and instructing their people. On the one hand they have ceaselessly condemned the injustice and oppression by which a large section of the population was afflicted, and again and again called on the Government to institute the necessary reforms. On the other hand they have repeatedly warned against the use of unlawful means in the attempt by the people to wrest

116

their legitimate rights from the authorities. These statements can be documented from a regular series of pronouncements by the Irish Bishops, individually and collectively, over a long period. To confine ourselves to roughly the hundred years preceding the present troubles in Northern Ireland, one may cite, for example, a meeting of the Hierarchy in May 1862, in which the Bishops declare that they are aware of injustices, but 'warn Catholics against all such combinations whether bound by oath or otherwise and especially against those which have for object to spread the spirit of revolution'. In the following year, on 4 August, 1863, the Hierarchy decided to 'condemn all such organisations' (e.g. the Brotherhood of St. Patrick) but also expressed their regret that the Government had not ameliorated the condition of the Irish.

Two decades later this standpoint of the Irish Catholic Bishops was referred to in approving terms by Pope Leo XIII. Addressing Cardinal McCabe and other Irish clerics in Rome in 1882, the Pope said : 'The Irish Bishops have not failed to point out to Catholics the path to follow, and to remind them that the praiseworthy intention of improving the condition of that country must not be separated from the love of justice and the employment of legitimate means'.

In 1897, in a pastoral letter written to mark the fiftieth anniversary of the death of Daniel O'Connell, Cardinal Logue set O'Connell up as a model for all Irishmen, inasmuch as he had united true patriotism with a love of the Church. In 1903, the Cardinal warned that 'patriotism never can carry us outside the bounds which the law of God prescribes'.

It is true that during the Fenian period individual

bishops, such as Archbishop MacHale of Tuam and Bishop Duggan of Clonfert, were very sympathetic to the Fenian cause. Nevertheless they too were essentially constitutionalists, but because they agreed so strongly with the Fenian aspiration for Irish freedom they could not be happy with any unqualified condemnation of the movement.

Indeed, so stern was the opposition of the Hierarchy as a body to the revolutionary groups that the doctrine of lawful revolt, which has long been accepted in Catholic theology, was pushed completely into the background. The tendency was, not only in Ireland but in Europe as a whole, to brand all revolution as unlawful, because of the atheistic and anti-Catholic bent of many revolutionaries. Against this background it is not surprising that, at the time of the 1916 rising, the attitude of the Hierarchy was one of opposition and disapproval. As the fighting spread throughout the country, however, and the populace was subjected to unjust and tyranous treatment by the forces of the Crown, various episcopal pronouncements condemned oppression and identified it as a cause of violence. 'We are not ruled by the ordinary law', said Cardinal Logue in 1919, 'but are subject to a drastic military code under which actions otherwise harmless or trivial become grave offences and are pitilessly punished'. In 1920 the Bishops laid the blame for violence on the Castle policy of oppression, but nonetheless condemned the violence. They went on to say, however, that the legitimate claim for self-government had been denied. In the period immediately following, both the Government policy of oppression and the recourse to violence were repeatedly condemned in episcopal statements. Speaking on 28 September, 1923, Archbishop Gilmartin of Tuam said : 'The Bishops had never condemned the Republican Ideal—what they had condemned was the use by any element of illegal force, the use, in other words, of unlawful means to override the people's will.'

In the period since the setting up of the Free State, the policy of the Bishops in regard to violence remained unchanged. In 1927 Cardinal O'Donnell complained that Catholics were still excluded from public office in Belfast, but the opposition to violence was a recurring theme in pastoral letters and other statements. In 1934 the Bishops in their Lenten Pastorals made a common appeal for the cessation of political hatreds, with their outcrop of outrages, murder and violence. In 1935, and again in 1940, illegal societies were condemned, the I.R.A. being specifically named in the latter year as 'a sinful and irreligious society'.

With the outbreak of a new campaign of violence in the North of Ireland in the mid-fifties, fresh con-demnations of unlawful recourse to arms were issued. In January 1956 the Standing Committee of the Hierarchy warned against 'erroneous ideas and claims which are being advanced in regard to the raising of military forces and the waging of war . . .' The Bishops went on to declare that 'it is a mortal sin for a Catholic to become or remain a member of an organisation or society which arrogates to itself the right to bear arms and use them against its own or another state'. On 25 December of the same year Cardinal D'Alton said : 'I wish to remind our young men that acts of violence will not advance the cause they have at heart'.

Since the outbreak of the recent troubles in the North the Hierarchy has persistently condemned violence, especially as represented by Cardinal Conway, and by the Bishops of Down and Connor and Ardagh and Clonmacnois. This condemnation has been both general and particular, whether in reference to the I.R.A., Protestant paramilitary groups, or crimes of the security forces. The factors contributing to the recourse to violence were also condemned — injustices, discrimination, one-sided application of penal measures.

Joint Statement by Catholic Bishops
21st May, 1970

The following statement has been issued by the Cardinal Archbishop of Armagh and by the Bishops of Derry, Dromore, Kilmore, Down & Connor and Clogher.

'In recent weeks many people have expressed anxiety about increasing violence in Northern Ireland. People are worried about the course events may take during the coming election campaign and throughout the summer. In these circumstances we feel it our duty to give expression to certain thoughts and moral principles which we know are already in the minds and hearts of our people as a whole.

'The overwhelming majority of our people do not want violence. They realise that it is morally wrong and that it is doubly so in Northern Ireland at the present time because of what it may lead to. It could lead to great suffering and death. It could lead to a repetition of the horrors we endured last Autumn and even worse. And, as always, the people who would suffer most are the innocent and the poor. The people who are mourning their dead of last August, the people who had to spend last winter in wooden shacks, know what violence leads to. The Catholic people as a whole abhor it.

'Since this is the case it would be a betrayal of the Catholic community—a stab in the back—for any individual, or group, to take it upon themselves to deliberately provoke violent incidents. So far as our people are concerned this would be quite a new turn of events but there is some evidence that it may have happened in recent days. If this is so then in the name of God and the whole Catholic community we condemn it.

'Such evil initiatives are contrary to the law of Christ and must bring harm to thousands of innocent people. Moreover if such acts can be pointed to as the beginning of serious trouble it is not the handful of self-appointed activists who will be blamed but the whole Catholic community. Already people are not above suggesting that what has happened in recent days convicts the Catholic community for what happened last August.

'It is no justification for such conduct to say that there was provocation or to say, even with some justice, that much worse deeds have been done by others and have gone unpunished. Two wrongs do not make a right.

'Already the effects of recent incidents are being felt in the strain and illness and economic pressure which innocent people are suffering. No one has the right to inflict a situation of this kind on the people.

'We therefore ask our people to make their voices heard in repudiation of individuals or groups who may appear to be interested in a continuation of violence. We ask them to co-operate with those groups who genuinely reflect the peaceful intentions of the people as a whole and who are working hard to restrain militant elements. We appeal in a particular way to the women—who are often the people who suffer most—and to parents. Your children could be maimed for life, psychologically and otherwise, by a continuation of these disturbances. There are many deep-seated wrongs to be undone in our society. Violence will only delay the day when they can be removed.

'Significant changes have taken place with regard to the position of the minority in Northern Ireland during the past eighteen months. We regard it as essential that the programme of reform be adhered to, without any deviation, and pursued to its logical conclusion of fair treatment for all, in face as well as in law. As these changes — and other vitally important changes which have been promised — take effect there will be a genuine prospect of justice and peace and further progress by orderly means. To anyone who thinks rationally about the future of the people concerned — and it is the people, human beings, that matter, not causes or ideologies—there can be no question of where the choice must lie between the violent way and the peaceful way. We warn those few individuals who would opt for the violent way that they have absolutely no mandate from the people.

'The principles of our Christian faith, which must be our supreme guide, powerfully reinforce the message of reason and common sense. Next to the love of God the greatest commandment is love of our neighbour. One neighbour, as the catechism teaches us, is "mankind of every description, even those who injure us or differ from us in religion". Most of our neighbours here are our fellow-

Christians, united with us in the love and worship of the same God and the same Lord and Saviour Jesus Christ.

'There may be moments when this most difficult of all commandments calls for almost superhuman restraint. Even then we are bound by it. If we have recourse to God in prayer he will not deny us the grace to be faithful to this His great commandment.'

Joint Statement by Catholic Bishops
12th September, 1971

The following statement has been issued by Cardinal Conway and the Bishops of Derry, Dromore, Kilmore, Down & Connor and Clogher :

'In the present dangerous situation in Northern Ireland it is important that people should see facts clearly. On a future occasion we may find it necessary to speak at some length on certain aspects of the present situation about which Catholics feel a very real sense of grievance. In this short statement, however, we wish to focus attention on one fact in particular. That is that in Northern Ireland at the present time there is a small group of people who are trying to secure a united Ireland by the use of force.

'One has only to state this fact in all its stark simplicity to see the absurdity of the idea. Who in his sane senses wants to bomb a million Protestants into a united Ireland ?

'At times the people behind this campaign will talk of "defence". But anyone who looks at the facts knows that it is not just defence. They themselves have admitted openly that they are engaged in offensive operations.

'Moreover their bombs have killed and maimed and terrorised innocent people, including women and girls. Their campaign is bringing shame and disgrace on noble and just causes. It is straining people's nerves to breaking point. It is destroying people's livelihood. It is intensifying sectarian bitterness. It is pushing the union of minds and hearts between men and women of all Ireland farther and farther away.

'All this because a handful of men, without any mandate from the people, have decided that this is the way to achieve a united Ireland. This is the way to postpone a really united Ireland until long after all Irish men and women now living are dead.

'We are well aware that this campaign of violence is not the sole cause of the present situation. We know as well as anyone the very real depression which the minority feels at the thought of having to live forever under a Government of the same political party as has ruled here for fifty years, the deep indignation which the recent internment swoops caused, the humiliation of innocent men, the allegations of brutality and worse, many of which we are convinced are well-founded. Many Protestants in Northern Ireland—good Christian people—will not like our mentioning these things. We ask them to realise that these facts are part of the total situation. What we want to emphasise is that we are painfully aware of these facts and *nevertheless* we condemn the violence. We also condemn the vicious evil of intimidation, from whatever source and on whatever side. This is a deadly poison which eats away at the very roots of personal freedom in society.

'We appeal also to Catholics to realise the

genuine fears and deep frustrations of the Protestant community at the present time. Understanding each other's fears and feelings can smooth the path to peace.

'The problems of this divided community will never be solved until a radical reform of the institutions of democracy here is introduced. Mathematical "majority-rule" simply does not work in a community of this kind.

'Our main purpose in this statement, however, is to repeat, unreservedly and without qualification, our condemnation of violence. Many of those engaged in it may be in good faith, confused by conflicting emotions and ideals. But the thing itself if grievously wrong and contrary to the law and spirit of Christ. Those responsible for it carry a grave responsibility of guilt before God.'

Joint Statement by Catholic Bishops
21st November, 1971

The following statement has been issued by Cardinal Conway and the Bishops of Derry, Dromore, Kilmore, Down & Connor and Clogher :

'During the past three years we have repeatedly declared our abhorrence of violence as a means to political ends. The trail of death and destruction still continues: murders, explosions in crowded places, destruction of public services and of business and industrial premises, intimidation, the humiliation of young girls and the demoralisation of youth. We declare once again that those who are responsible, directly or indirectly, for these things are bringing shame and disgrace on noble and just causes and are acting contrary to the law of Christ. We condemn in a special way some particularly cold-blooded murders in recent weeks.

'It is also our duty, however, to condemn another form of violence which is also shameful and contrary to the law of Christ. We refer to the process known as "interrogation in depth" as it has been practised in Northern Ireland in recent months. Men have been kept hooded and standing, with arms and legs outstretched, practically continuously for days and nights on end until, from exhaustion (leading to repeated collapses), darkness, noise and thirst, they felt they were going out of their minds and prayed for death.

'These were men who had been imprisoned without trial. One of them who suffered most has since been released.

'We condemn this treatment as immoral and inhuman. It is unworthy of the British people. It is the test of a civilised people that the methods of its elected government remain civilised even under extreme provocation.

'We have also disturbing medical evidence of the physical beating of arrested persons even in recent weeks.

'People will never understand the terrible situation here until they appreciate the intense bitterness which excessive or unjust methods of repression engender throughout a whole community.

'We cannot emphasise too strongly our conviction that the solution to our present tragic situation will never be found in violence or counter-violence. Far-reaching political initiatives must be sought as a matter of great urgency if those who advocate violence are to be deprived of their chief ally—despair.'

Bibliography

Violence and Civil Disturbances in Northern Ireland in 1969; Report of Tribunal of Inquiry CMD 566 (N.I.) 2 vols. Belfast HMSO 1972 (The Scarman Report).

Housing Intimidation in Belfast. Community Relations Commission, 1973.

Disturbances in Northern Ireland; report of the Commission appointed by the Governor of Northern Ireland. CMD 532 (N.I.) Belfast HMSO 1969 (The Cameron Commission).

Report of the Advisory Committee on Police in Northern Ireland CMD 535 (N.I.) Belfast HMSO 1969 (The Hunt Report).

Report of the Allegations against the Security Forces of Physical Brutality in Northern Ireland, arising out of the events on 9th August, 1971 CMD 4823 London HMSO 1971 (The Compton Report).

British Army and Special Branch RUC Brutalities; December 1971 - February 1972. D. Faul and R. Murray, Cavan 1972.

Report of the Committee of Privy Counsellors appointed to consider Unauthorised Procedures for the Interrogation of Persons suspected of Terrorism. CMD 4901 London HMSO 1972 (The Parker Report).

Report of a Committee to consider, in the Context of Civil Liberties and Human Rights, Measures to Deal with Terrorism in Northern Ireland. CMD 5847. London HMSO 1975 (The Gardiner Report).

H. A. Lyons *The Psychological Effects of the Civil Disturbances on Children.* The Northern Teacher. Winter 1973.

M. Fraser *Children in Conflict.* Pelican Books, 1973, and articles in New Society, April 15th, 1971, reprinted in Community Forum No. 2, 1972.

Children's Play, Ruth Overy—part of a symposium Community Forum, No. 2, 1972.

Corrymeela, The Search for Peace, Alf McCreary, Christian Journals Ltd., Belfast.

Ireland's Conflict Diminishes Me, Stephen G. Mackie, British Council of Churches.

The Working Party

Joint Chairmen

The Most Reverend Cahal B. Daly, Bishop of Ardagh and Clonmacnois.

The Reverend Dr. R. D. Eric Gallagher.

Members

Mr. Denis P. Barritt

The Rt. Hon. David W. Bleakley

The Reverend Robert N. Brown

Mr. Jerome Connelly

The Reverend Dr. Michael Crowe (unable to attend in 1976 because of absence abroad)

Professor Norman J. Gibson

The Very Reverend Dr. James L. M. Haire

Miss Kathleen Kelly

The Reverend Michael McGrail

The Reverend Dr. Kevin McNamara

The Reverend Columb O'Donnell (resigned on transfer)

Dr. A. Stanley Worrall